Amber Waves
of Grain

Third in the Series of Stories
about Growing Up in and
Around Small Towns in the Midwest

Edited by Jean Tennant

Shapato Publishing
Everly, Iowa

Published by: Shapato Publishing
PO Box 476
Everly, IA 51338

ISBN: 978-0-9826992-6-3

Library of Congress Control Number: 2010934928
Copyright © 2010 Shapato Publishing

First Printing October 2010
Cover photo provided by Carolyn Rohrbaugh
Artwork by LaVonne M. Hansen

ACKNOWLEDGMENTS

A couple of years ago I decided to put together a collection of personal experience essays about life in the Midwest. The result was *Walking Beans Wasn't Something You Did With Your Dog*, an anthology containing thirty true stories by authors from a variety of states. I honestly thought it would be a one-time project, but I underestimated the popularity of these stories and how hungry people are to read of former times when living was simpler—though inarguably much harder. The success of the book prompted me to gather stories for a sequel, and in 2009 Shapato Publishing produced a second anthology, titled *Knee High by the Fourth of July*. That second volume contains thirty-three stories, but still I was forced to reject several excellent pieces . . . which made it easy to plan the third book in the series.

Amber Waves of Grain features thirty-eight stories, by some repeat authors and many new. It's always exciting for me to discover a fresh voice to share, in my own small way, with the world.

As with the earlier volumes, this one has been very much a joint effort. The patience and encouragement of my husband and business partner, Grover Reiser, kept me going through the long hours and many late nights. The endless editing sessions became more fun than formidable by working with my tireless friend, Betty Taylor, whose "From Amber Waves to Threshing Days" is the first story in this book. She's always there when I need her. And her husband, Orville Taylor, with his knowledge of farming, among other things, has kept us on the straight and narrow. On more than one occasion, he saved us from the embarrassment of printing things that weren't quite accurate.

Thank you, all of you.

Jean Tennant

CONTENTS

Acknowledgments   v

From Amber Waves to Threshing Days   1
    Betty Taylor

Detasseling   7
    Bonnie Ewoldt

Buried in Berries   11
    Beverley Haney

Michigan Farmers' Market   13
    Cindy Reynolds

My Mother's Treadle Sewing Machine
and my Yarn-Haired Doll   17
    Carolyn Rohrbaugh

The Cook Stove   21
    Arlene Walker

I Wish I had my Sunbonnet   27
    Marilyn Kratz

Ingenuity   29
    Marie Wells

Finding my Heart in the Heartland   35
    Jean Tennant

City Girl View   39
    Rebecca Groff

The Singing Silo   45
Karen J. Schutt

Curly Hair   51
Mary Berdan

Little Red Stomping Hood   53
Keith Jensen

Love of Words Began in a Single Room   59
Ruth Hunziker Underhill

The Bus   63
Leslie Means

Six-on-Six   69
Judy Taber

Blizzard Days   73
Verla Klaessy

The Blizzard of 1975 – A Near Cat . . . astrophe   77
Roger Stoner

Journey Through the Valley of Death   83
Pat Larsen

He Knew   89
Irene Jaeger

The Hired Man   93
Marilyn Ford

My Friend Elmer 97
Isaiah Gray

Bottle Lamb to Bunting Buck 101
Delores Swanson

Of Old Dogs and Men 107
H. "Bumper" Bauer

No Pets Allowed 111
Terry Overocker

Dad and the Christmas Opossum 115
Mark Smith

Mama and the Rattlesnake 119
Ed Stevens

Coming Through, Wilma! 125
C. R. Lindemer

Cane Pole Logic 129
R. C. Davis

What's in a Name? 135
Gene Miller

Ode to a Road Less Taken 139
Rae Rogers

Leaving Home 141
Joyce Jenkins

Hometown Gratitude   147
    Andrea Bean

Remembering the Greats   151
    Francis Menenga

November 22, 1963   155
    Karen Laughlin

Scrapbooks   161
    Ruth Jochims

A Box Full of Memories   165
    Delpha Chouanard

The Back Porch   169
    Ronda Armstrong

Photo provided by Barbara Haack

FROM AMBER WAVES TO THRESHING DAYS

Betty Taylor

Iowa farms of the thirties and forties possessed a charm greater than that of today's rural landscape. Horses, cattle, and sheep idled beside tree-lined streams. Cornfields lay in rows, perfectly checked to accommodate cross cultivating for weed control. Hay and small-grain fields created geometric patterns around them. The artistry of Grant Wood preserved the scenery of the era in paintings such as *Spring in the Country, Young Corn,* and *Fall Plowing.*

As spring growth emerged, my father could tell by varied shades of green whether crops were oats, flax, barley, or different varieties of hay. In July, small-grain began to "head out," or form seeds, and I could see that Dad was invariably right about crop identification.

Flax fields bloomed with flowers of purest blue, dotting the countryside with what looked like small rectangular lakes. As July wore on, ripening crops turned from green to varied shades of amber. Flax was the darkest; its blue blossoms had gradually evolved into brown orbs filled with golden seeds. Oats matured first, followed by barley, and finally the flax.

In late July or early August, Dad hitched his horses to a binder that would cut the ripened grain, bind it into bundles, and toss them onto a cradle at the side of the machine. When there were six or eight bundles in the cradle, he tripped a foot pedal to drop them to the ground. They would later be made into shocks.

Dad and my brothers could pick up one bundle in each hand and deftly set them together as they created six-bundle shocks. Later, Dad taught me to make five-bundle shocks, firmly setting one down with both hands and arranging the other four around it. They needed to be solid enough to avoid leaning and slanted enough to shed rain. If the straw became wet, farmers had to [1]tip the shocks so they could dry out before [2]threshing.

Fathers and sons worked together in "threshing rings" of about eight neighbors. One man owned a machine designed to separate grain from straw. Their wives planned hearty meals. Since there was no electricity for refrigeration, much of the food needed to be prepared on the day it was served. Some women worked together or hired neighbor girls, but many had daughters to help cook, bake, and wait tables.

While Dad threshed with neighbors, Mom contemplated her turn to cook. Conscious of fixing something different from what other wives had prepared, she frequently asked what he'd had for dinner. The question annoyed him; he thought it mattered little if meals were the same as long as they were ample.

When we were about ten and seven, Esther and I would watch for Dad to come home from threshing with neighbors. He smiled indulgently when we ran out to meet him, stopped his horses, and we climbed aboard the rack.

"Bend your knees a bit," he'd say. "It'll even out the ride."

With one of us on each side of him, we chattered about the day's events. Once I emulated my mother's question. "What did you have for dinner?"

"Skunk, 'possum, and turnips," he replied.

Uneven jolts from the iron-tired wheels, plus our odd stance, jiggled my laughter on the pleasant ride home.

I knew he'd be relieved that his chores were finished. We had giggled when Mom traded her housedress and apron for Dad's bibbed overalls and went to the barn with my brother, Gordon, to milk the cows by hand. At eleven, he was still too young to work in the ring.

Excitement filled the air on the day the horse-drawn racks began to arrive. They were finishing a neighbor's field and ready to start on ours. [3]A large tractor towing the threshing machine pulled in last. The owner positioned them carefully at the work site, blocked their wheels, and oiled all moving parts. The mechanism that would separate grain from straw operated through a series of pulleys, belts, and gears. The longest belt connected the machine to the tractor that powered everything from about thirty-five feet away. With the engine running, it gathered momentum, and the machine hummed into action as racks filled with bundles began to roll in from the field.

Haulers positioned loads on either side of the rig and began pitching bundles into a hopper. Grain poured from a spout into grain wagons. Two men watched the wagons, exchanged them, and elevated the grain into a bin. Straw spewed from a blower. Pitchfork in hand and working in the chaff, Dad built a straw stack designed to shed rain while my brothers, Bob and Arnold, managed his teams and pitched bundles.

Under the big cottonwood tree in the corner of the yard, Esther and I set up a washstand with a basin, soap, and towels. The laborers could fill the basin at a nearby hand pump and wash up before dinner at noon. At times, one of the fellows would bend over, stick his head under the spout, and pump water to cool his head and neck and get rid of some of the chaff.

While Mom and my oldest sister, Marge, were busily cooking, we younger ones opened the big round oak table as far as we could, added leaves, covered it with oilcloth, and set places for as many men as possible. Tempting odors filled the house. Potatoes were staples for every meal. They could be scalloped, mashed, creamed, or made into potato salad and served with pot roast, ham, pork chops, or fried chicken—but never skunk, 'possum, or turnips. The menu also included garden vegetables, pickles, homemade rolls, jams, and jellies. Generous portions of apple, cherry, or butterscotch pies were served for dessert.

After the men unloaded the last of the morning bundles, they watered their horses and fed them oats from boxes built onto the backs of their hayracks. One by one, the neighbors entered our house for well-deserved meals and removed their straw hats to reveal "farmers' tans." Protected foreheads were white, but the rest of their faces were tanned to a copper brown. Pleasant conversations were exchanged around the dining table.

When finished, they rose one by one to make room for someone else, picked up their hats, and turned to my mother with polite comments like, "Thanks, Mrs. Hembd," "Much obliged for the nice meal," or "Everything was real good."

Mom looked pleased. The comments were sincere. Her meal was a success. Quickly we re-set the empty places with clean dishes. The man who ran the rig and my father, who'd been stacking straw, ate last. With appetites satisfied, the guys might rest on the lawn a bit, but soon they headed for the field to get loads ready by the time the threshing machine would be humming again.

As soon as we finished clearing the table and washing dishes, we prepared mid-afternoon lunches. Mom had purchased bread, sausage or baloney, and cheese. Bread from the store was a treat and easier to use for making sandwiches that would be served with homemade cake or cookies.

Even on hot days, Mom made coffee in addition to cold drinks. Esther and I took on the tedious job of reaming lemons for lemonade. If the Watkins van had stopped recently, we might make Watkins cherry or orange nectar. Around mid-afternoon, many hands carried those refreshments to the work site to be placed on a platform beside the water bucket and dipper.

One afternoon a neighbor girl came to play with me during threshing time. We were upstairs when the phone rang. Audrey's mother was calling to say that her daughter shouldn't start home because a hobo was coming down the road. We watched from a window as he approached, turned up our drive, and knocked on the door. Mom shooed us away before she went to the door to give him a drink and some of the sandwiches she had prepared for the threshers. He sat at the end of our drive, ate his food, and headed down the road again.

After several days at our place, the men proceeded to another farm in the ring. When everyone's oats and barley were finished, crews returned to thresh the flax. Later, the owner of the rig held a "settle-up" meeting at his place. The farmers came to pay their bills, but whole families attended. We played with the other children until time for cookies, cake, and homemade ice cream.

The excitement of threshing days had ended. I never heard my mother complain about them, but those days must have been more difficult than exciting for her.

One summer, my husband and I went to the Dubuque Museum of Art to attend a Grant Wood exhibit. *American Gothic*, Wood's most noted painting was there on loan, and I wanted to see the original. It was intriguing, but for me *The Threshing Table* eclipsed all of his other paintings.

My eyes misted at the familiar sight—hard-working men at the table, decent neighbors with white foreheads and brown faces. I knew they would be visiting good-naturedly until one by one they'd leave the table, pick up their straw hats, thank the woman of the house for the good meal, and rest on the lawn a bit before returning to the fields.

[1] The woman and children on the cover are taking a rest after "tipping shocks." The youngest boy is sitting on a tipped shock and two of the boys in bibbed overalls are holding tools used for the job.

[2] The terms thrash and thrashing were used in my early years. Thrash means "to beat or flail." Thresh means "to separate grain from straw."

[3] Earl Langel of Milford, Iowa, who frequents threshing events, was my resource for threshing details, and my husband, Orville Taylor, corrected several of my misconceptions.

Betty Taylor was planted and nourished among the grain fields of northwest Iowa. She has traveled throughout the United States and Canada as well as other areas of the world. The best segment of each journey has been the one that returns to her home area, filled with rich and grounding memories.

Photo provided by Barbara Haack

DETASSELING

Bonnie Ewoldt

We were penniless 15-year-olds in the '60s when my cousin talked me into signing on with a detasseling crew. At a dollar per hour, plus a ten-cent-per-hour bonus for finishing the two-week season, detasseling paid good money. It was seasonal work that needed to be completed in a timely manner before seed corn self-pollinated. How hard could this be— walking through corn rows, pulling out tassels? By the time she finished her sales pitch, there wasn't a doubt in my mind that we would complete the season with $100 in our pockets.

After meeting the crew at 5:00 AM, I soon began to doubt this latest get-rich-quick scheme. We were loaded into the back of a ton-and-a-half Chevy straight truck with an old, green, army-surplus tarp providing shelter from the morning chill. The foreman rode in the cab while the crew sat in the box on planks that wobbled on concrete blocks.

The smell of the mildewed tarp hung in the air as grinding gears set the truck in motion to rumble out of town. When we turned onto a gravel road, dust began sifting through the cracks of the box and billowing in through the opening at the back. By the time we reached the cornfield I was coughing and sweating and more than ready to turn around and go home.

Unfortunately, at that point, I had no idea where home was, having ridden in the back of a dusty, windowless truck for over an hour. For all I knew, we had driven directly to Hades.

After brief instructions from the gruff and burly foreman, we were assigned to cornrows. I squinted up against the sun and gazed at the tassels waving far above me. Looking ahead, I peered into a dark tunnel of corn leaves, tips touching across the rows. I sighed. There was nothing left to do but plunge in and start trudging through the dense green jungle.

Within minutes, my "cheery outlook" digressed even further as I became entangled in the cold, wet leaves of crisp, dew-covered cornstalks. Only a few feet into the row, I was soaked to the skin and covered with pollen. I soon discovered it was no easy task to walk and constantly reach overhead to find tassels. After several feeble attempts and a few broken stalks, I finally figured out how to wrestle one toward me. I could then grasp, twist, and dislodge the tassel, bend sideways to keep the leaves from slapping my face, and release the stalk to spring back into place.

Since I was not wearing gloves, my hands became covered with slimy "goo" from the base of the tassels. My feet became heavier with each step as mud from the irrigated field oozed into my shoes. As I was wearing only shorts and a sleeveless shirt, dressing for the temperature, not the job, by the end of the day my arms and legs bore numerous slash marks from razor-sharp corn leaves and my neck and face became sunburned.

The hot July sun burned off the morning dew, and my body temperature went from shivering to sweltering. After walking for what seemed like miles, we finally reached the end of the row and were given a water break. I filled a cup full of water from the galvanized Igloo cooler and collapsed in the shade of the nearest cornstalk, keenly aware of aches in every inch of my tired body. The reprieve was short-lived. All too soon, the foreman had us back on our feet and moving. By lunchtime I was hungrier than I could ever remember being. My meager lunch—an apple, sandwich, and cookie—hardly made a dent in the hunger pangs.

In the early afternoon, when the sun was high above our heads and the temps were heading into the nineties, we climbed back into the truck and headed home. When that old Chevy screeched to a stop, I jumped out and informed my cousin that I'd had enough! Bonus or no bonus, there was no way I would face another day of torture!

That proclamation did not deter my never-take-no-for-an-answer cousin and, after some arm-twisting and comments about being "a quitter," I agreed to try one more day.

With a good night's rest, adequate lunch, and job-appropriate clothing of jeans, hat, gloves, and my dad's long-sleeved shirt, I survived the next day . . . and the next and the next. Before I knew it, the two weeks were finished and the detasseling season had come to an end.

When our $115 paychecks arrived in the mail, our moms took us shopping for school clothes in Omaha. Two weeks' pay disappeared in one day, and I enjoyed spending every penny of it!

After a year to reflect, I decided detasseling wasn't *that* bad and signed on for another season.

Bonnie Boeck Ewoldt recently retired from teaching at-risk high school students. She grew up on a farm near Denison, Iowa, and currently lives with her husband on an acreage near the Iowa Great Lakes. She is a freelance writer and motivational speaker. Her work has appeared in *Country* and *Country Extra* magazines.

Photo provided by Beverley Haney

BURIED IN BERRIES

Beverley Haney

Picking blueberries was one of my favorite summertime tasks. And the reason I loved it was because I got to do it with my Mom, alone. As the youngest of seven, I was always competing for Mom's attention. Berry picking together had become a yearly routine for the two of us and I happily looked forward to having my mom all to myself.

I would hitch my chestnut-colored pony, Dolly, to the two-wheeled cart, and Mom and I, dressed in bib overalls for the occasion, would toss our metal pails over the wooden wheels, and then climb up onto the wooden bench.

Off we would go, about a half-mile down the road to the "bush," our little cart raising a trail of dust behind us as we rattled over the dirt road. Mickey, our collie, trotted along beside us, occasionally darting off to chase a gopher back down its hole.

The bush consisted mostly of oak trees, as well as the fruit-laden blueberry bushes, while lacey willows lined the little creek that ran through the middle. The willows harbored great swarms of mosquitoes and we wore the overalls and long-sleeved shirts to try to impede their bloodthirsty progress.

We tossed the buckets over the side and climbed down after them. I tied Dolly to a tree and she happily began to graze on the tall grass. Mickey darted to and fro, excitedly exploring the new smells all around her.

Mom quickly made her way to the best bushes and soon there was a rhythmic, metallic plunk, plunk, plunk as the purple fruit hit the bottom of her pail. I followed suit, dragging my pail along as I tried to match her steady rhythm. However, I was as easily distracted as our collie and I would be off, running barefoot through the creek, hopping from stone to stone. Soon those pesky mosquitoes would get the best of me and I would run back to Mom.

The morning sped by as we chatted and laughed and filled our pails. At noon we found a comfortable log to sit on as we ate our peanut butter and jelly sandwiches and shared drinks of water from an old canning jar wrapped in paper to keep it cold.

By afternoon our pails were filled and we hoisted them back into the cart and were ready to head home. We hated to leave the cool shade of the bush for the hot prairie sun.

I flicked the reins and Dolly trotted forward. To get back onto the road we had to go down through a ditch and up onto the road.

Apparently I steered the cart at a sharp angle, and we flipped over. The next thing we knew, we were lying on the ground, the buckets of blueberries scattered in the dirt all around us and many squashed beneath us. Dolly stood there patiently. Her harness was pulled over sideways and one of the cart's shafts rested on top of her back, but she was none the worse for wear.

As soon as we determined that none of us was hurt, Mom and I looked at each other, appreciating how ridiculous we looked lying on the ground covered with purple blotches, and we began to giggle. As we proceeded to right the cart and brush off the dirt and berries from each other, we laughed harder and harder.

We laughed all the way home, arriving empty-handed, our clothes a mess. Though it didn't end up very productive, for me it created another wonderful memory of a day I got to spend with my mom.

Beverley Haney lives in Evergreen, Colorado, and winters in Mesa, Arizona. Besides writing, her other creative outlet is playing fiddle in a bluegrass band with her husband Jim.

MICHIGAN FARMERS' MARKET

Cindy Reynolds

Saturday mornings in June were always reserved for our weekly shopping trips to the Farmers' Market. Five of us kids would all pile into the family station wagon, sans seatbelts, with our doggie, Sam, sticking his head out the side window. The car ride was often silent, as Mom navigated the bumpy ride along rural roads.

Farmland, silos, and animals dotted the passing countryside.

Pulling into the dirt-paved parking lot, I could see farmers in overalls unloading their fresh produce from the rear of their pickup trucks. Their wives, with brightly colored print aprons and with their hair wrapped in netting, carefully lifted baskets filled with flowers and baked goods.

Mom gave each of us a recycled bag to shop with, long before the world became "green." She told us to select only the freshest homegrown goods in our designated shopping area, and then she gave us each a few dollars to spend and sent us off in different directions.

It was only later in life that I realized Mom had been providing us with an early lesson in how to shop wisely and healthfully.

I remember visiting the flower stalls on a Saturday morning. The beautifully colored blossoms and leaves were like a painting of paradise. I decided to choose my favorite annual, and with the help of a farmhand I carried away the most brilliant bouquet of sunflowers. They were bursting with color and their huge, sunny faces supported by thick stems, dwarfed my twelve-year old frame.

On another Saturday, Mom gave me the job of shopping for fresh fruit. The farmers at the counter let me sample their summer varieties. I so loved the Michigan red cherries, juicy and sweet, that I almost forgot there were seeds in the middle.

They left a scarlet red stain on my hands, which remained with me for a few days. I sampled the plump, ripened straw-berries, consuming more than I cared to count. The farmer should have put me on the weigh scale, along with the container of strawberries that I eventually purchased.

Across the aisle, I watched as my brother selected fresh bread from the bakery lady. The bakery lady sat behind her booth, knitting something special for someone, with a contented smile on her face. Settled in at her post for the day, she crossed her legs at the ankles and was never bothered by requests for samples. The sweet smell of buttery bread and cookies wafted down that whole row of the market.

I met up with my sister, Linda, at the vegetable stand. She had already bought green beans, lettuce and fresh herbs. As the farmer handed her a bag of new potatoes, I noticed the dirt beneath his fingernails. It made me think about the physical labor that a farmer endures—tilling the soil, planting the crops, making sure the ground stays moist in the event of a drought. Then he must reap the fruits of his labor, package them to transport to market, and sell them at farm stands, grocery stores and food warehouses.

The realization that the farmer's livelihood depended on the success of his crops imprinted a picture in my mind; the good earth provides us with a healthy bounty to sustain our lives. Growing up in the Great Lakes state provided our large, growing family the opportunity to enjoy farm fresh food, grown locally.

I can still hear Mom's voice drawing me out of my morning reverie. She'd give her signature "Call of the Wild," and her children would appear from all different directions, shopping bags in hand. The traces of crumbs and colors around our mouths revealed the generous samples provided by the farmers.

All of the morning purchases were carefully placed in a large, rectangular basket on the back seat of our car. My two older sisters and I would call "first dibs" to sit in the far back seat of our family station wagon.

The ride home was filled with lively chatter about our morning adventures at the market. Our doggie would stick his head out the window, taking in gulps of farm fresh air and watching the passing scenery.

Looking back on this treasured memory, I realize that we were living the good life, here on Earth.

Cindy Reynolds lives in the Boston area with her husband, two college-aged sons and toy poodle, Meggie. She runs her own tutoring business and works as an historical tour guide with student exchange groups in the New England area. She has also authored the book *The Pinewood Derby* by Mirror Publishing.

Author on right with sister, Linda

Photo provided by Cindy Reynolds

Photo provided by Carolyn Rohrbaugh

MY MOTHER'S TREADLE SEWING MACHINE
AND MY YARN-HAIRED DOLL

Carolyn Rohrbaugh

The memory of my mother sitting at her treadle sewing machine is etched into my mind. I wanted to learn to sew, even as a little girl of five. Not only did she make and mend most of our clothes, she sewed strips of cloth together for our grandparents to make rugs in their rug shop. Most exciting of all were the May baskets she made from nut cups and machine ruffled crepe paper with pipe-cleaner handles. When she opened the sewing machine I was always there to watch. I sucked my thumb until I was seven, so sitting and watching and sucking was easy to do.

The Sears, Roebuck and Montgomery Ward catalogs and magazines were the main sources of our shopping. Once I saw a pattern for a yarn-haired doll in a magazine and told Mother I would like to have her. Before I knew it, the pattern arrived in the mail and she started making my doll.

Mother didn't always have time to work on my doll, but I watched each time as she cut it out, sewed the pieces together, stuffed it and finally added the yarn hair and clothes. My precious doll was then tucked into the bedding box in the back of my closet for safekeeping. After school I couldn't get to that bedding box fast enough. It was just my doll, my thumb and the bedding box until Mother would call for me to change my clothes and help with the chores.

My sister, Darla, who didn't suck her thumb, liked having parties, especially birthday parties. I was too busy sucking my thumb to worry about such things, but my parents were determined to make me give up the thumb. They would swab bad tasting medicine on it and say, "She won't suck that off," but it only took a minute or two to suck it off and all would be well with the world again.

For some long-forgotten reason I decided a seven-year birthday party would be nice. My parents made a bargain with me—a birthday party for giving up the thumb. It was a struggle, but the thumb sucking stopped. The birthday part was probably nice, but I don't even remember it.

My yarn-haired doll was still a treasure to me, but without my thumb she didn't seem quite so important. Her plight in life was the bedding box.

Then one day after school I ran to the bedding box. My doll had been ignored long enough. But she wasn't there. I ran to Mother and cried, "Where's my doll?"

She seemed surprised that I still cared. She said, "You didn't pay attention to her anymore so when I cleaned she went to the burn barrel." Because we lived in a very small house and the family was growing, Mother didn't keep anything that wasn't necessary. She was always cleaning, but still it seemed unbelievable that after she worked so long to make my doll, that she would just burn her.

My heart was broken.

After I was married, my mother updated to an electric sewing machine and gave me the old treadle. I made many clothes, costumes and yarn-haired dolls on that machine. When the day came that I updated to an electric sewing machine, I sold that precious treadle sewing machine for $5.

Now I wonder how I could have done that. Once again, my heart is broken.

Carolyn Rohrbaugh is retired and is enjoying having more time for family, friends, and writing. She loves tending her flowers, riding motorcycle with her husband, Bill, and writing her memories.

Photo provided by Arlene Walker

THE COOK STOVE

Arlene Walker

Some of my best childhood memories took place around the cook stove in our farmhouse kitchen. Huge and heavy, it kept us warm and cooked our meals as long as someone remembered to fuel the fire. Those were the days before any of the farms in our neighborhood were wired for electricity.

Dad's chair stood on one side of the stove near a window where he sat after dinner at noon. He'd listen to the news on the radio or read his daily paper before it was time to go out and hitch up the team of horses to work in the field. Needing no invitation, I'd climb on his lap and play with his watch. Attached to a piece of leather on one end and a buttonhole on the other, it was kept in a pocket in the bib of his overalls. I liked to hold the watch near my ear to hear it tick.

Meanwhile, Mom cleared the table. Then she'd dip hot water from the reservoir on the right side of the stove into a large white enamel pan. The copper-lined reservoir was kept filled with rainwater that was pumped into a pail in the kitchen sink and carried to the reservoir. The cistern was replenished whenever it rained. Rain flowed from the roof, spilling into eaves troughs, which emptied first into down-spouts and then into the cistern.

After Mom washed the dishes, she washed the black, cast iron pan. Mom used that pan for much of the cooking—pancakes, scrambled eggs, pork chops, fried potatoes, and more. I watched her closely, eager for the day when I would be able to work at the stove. In the meantime, Mom made a place on a pantry shelf for my tea set so I could have a pretend tea party. When I invited my brother to join me at my small table, he showed no interest.

A big aluminum teakettle, filled with well water, stood on the stove at all times, so that hot water would be available for cooking or brewing tea and coffee. The crackling of the fire accompanied by the humming of the teakettle was a song of contentment even when the wind howled outside.

Like a monster, our cook stove consumed all it was fed. At least once a day the metal cob box that stood on the left side of the stove had to be filled. If the fire went out, kerosene and a match on top of cobs or kindling were used to restart it.

Dad chopped dead branches that fell from trees in the grove and stacked the logs against one of the outbuildings until they were needed to feed the fire. A wood log burned longer than cobs. Dad also stored a small supply of coal purchased in town. Whenever we'd be gone for half a day or so, he'd put a piece of the coal in the fire so it would burn long and slow until we got home.

Waste paper was disposed of by lifting a lid directly over the fire and tossing it in. We children watched as flames licked the words away before the paper crumpled into a fragile black sheet and disintegrated into ashes.

Once, my sister pulled a pair of high-heeled shoes from a box of discarded garments, put them on her tiny feet and clomp-clomped around the house. Dad and Mom reminded her that wearing those shoes could damage her feet. When she paid no heed to the warnings, Dad confiscated the shoes, lifted the lid of the stove, and dropped them into the fire.

When my brother, my sister, and I were old enough, it became our chore to bring in cobs. Sometimes we were sent into the pig yard with a basket to pick up cobs left from the ears of corn Dad fed the pigs. Pigs cared nothing about cleanliness and they left a strong, unpleasant odor on any-thing in their environment. When we complained about handling those smelly cobs, Mom told us they made an especially good fire, but we knew better. It was more fun to carry an empty basket into the grove, where we stopped frequently to play on junked machinery. It took a long time to fill our basket with sticks of wood for kindling, but we did enjoy our adventures.

On winter nights, popcorn or hot chocolate around the cozy fire in the stove were bedtime treats. When it was time, we reluctantly left the warmth around the stove and went up to our cold bedrooms. Flannel sheets and a pile of covers locked in our body heat for a comfortable night's sleep.

When I woke up early, I'd hear Dad open the firebox downstairs to feed the fire. Covering as much of my head as I could without cutting off air to breathe, I'd luxuriate in the warmth until Dad called through the register in the floor, telling us it was time to get up.

On Sunday nights Mom pumped pail after pail of water from the pump over the sink. She filled the oval-shaped, copper boiler set on top of the stove. This water was soft, just right for washing our clothes. On Monday morning, after the boiler of water had heated, Mom did the laundry in the wringer washer and rinsed each piece in two rinse tubs that contained cold water.

On Saturday nights we took turns, from the youngest to the oldest, bathing in front of the stove in a round, metal tub— all in the same water.

During the winter, our cook stove seldom made the house too warm. However, during the summer, the heat from the cook stove raised the temperature to an unbearable dis-comfort. One summer, Dad recruited help and built a summer kitchen in the yard not far from the house. My parents purchased a second stove for summer cooking. By this time Mom trusted me to stir the soup or test boiling potatoes for doneness. One summer day she gave me permission to bake cookies from a recipe I'd copied from a magazine. While she finished some work in the house, I took out the mixing bowl and the metal spoon. While measuring and mixing sugar, shortening, and eggs, I felt confident, knowing the cookies would be good. But before I'd finished measuring the flour, I discovered that the stove was not hot enough for baking. I stirred the hot coals and added more cobs. Distracted by the interruption, I realized that while stirring the dough I'd measured and mixed in twice the amount of flour the recipe called for.

We were living in the aftermath of the Great Depression. Consequently, throwing the batch of dough away was not an option. My parents had learned to live frugally and had instilled in me that anything that had a use should not be discarded. There was only one solution to my dilemma. Lifting the large metal bread bowl from where it hung on a nail in the wall, I measured the same amount of sugar, shortening and eggs as I had mixed in the first batch. Then I added the first batch from the mixing bowl and stirred the now-double batch of dough.

I knew at least one family member who would appreciate having twice as many cookies. My brother was always hungry when he came in from helping Dad with the fieldwork or the chores. It took most of the morning to bake that double batch. When he saw the huge stack of cookies cooling, the grin on his face made up for my mistake in measuring the ingredients.

A few years after that, I graduated from high school and went off to college to become a teacher. My brother served our country in the military for several years. My sister took a job several hundred miles away. Our younger brother's college education was interrupted so he could serve in active duty in Vietnam. When we all gathered at the farm home, our lives had changed. Mom's life had changed too. No longer did she and Dad have to gather fuel and feed the fire. The cook stove no longer stood in its dominant place in the kitchen. It had been replaced with a gas-burning stove for cooking. A furnace heated the house that had been wired for electricity. Lights hung from all the ceilings and plug-ins provided energy for the latest appliances that were intended to make life easier.

Some things haven't changed. The memories of growing up around that cook stove taught us how to live and form bonds that modern conveniences and technology cannot take away.

Arlene Walker grew up on a farm in northwest Iowa. She has taught elementary grades, English Language Learners, and substituted in many school classrooms. Now retired, she writes full time. Her published work includes real life experiences and devotionals. She has also written and published stories and puzzles for children.

Photo provided by Arlene Walker

Photo provided by Judy Peters

I WISH I HAD MY SUNBONNET

Marilyn Kratz

I hated that sunbonnet when I was a girl. It felt like a helmet on sweltering summer days, but Mama insisted my sisters and I wear those contraptions from early morning till supper time. In the evenings, as the sun made its way down in the west and the shelter belt of fully-leafed elms shaded the entire farm yard, we were allowed to run around outside with our braids freely flopping.

It wasn't that Mama worried we'd some day end up with skin cancer. And she didn't even think about the fact that tanned skin wrinkles faster as we age. No, those matters didn't bother Mama. She had just one worry—freckles! Mama had lots of them herself, and she was determined her daughters would not.

So each year, before the first sunny days of summer, Mama sewed us each a new sunbonnet. We chose the fabric we wanted from her scrap box. Often our bonnets were made from two or three different pieces of scraps, making them unique and colorful.

Mama started by cutting a rectangle of two layers of fabric which would extend from the back of the head to about five inches beyond the face. She stitched tunnels in it and stuffed them with ribs of cardboard cut from old shoe boxes. I sometimes wonder where she found enough cardboard for all our bonnets since we certainly didn't get that many new shoes.

The cardboard-stiffed rectangle was held in shape around the face by sewing on more fabric covering the back of the head, extending down to the bottom of the neck and all the way around to the sides of the face. Mama sewed on two ribbons for us to tie at the back to keep the bonnets from sliding ahead and two more to tie under our chins to keep the relentless prairie wind from blowing the bonnets off.

I suppose I appreciated my bonnet on days when my sisters and I worked for hours under the sweltering skies, stacking oat bundles into shocks. They also helped keep the edges of cornstalk leaves from cutting into our faces as we walked the rows picking cockleburs. But those bonnets were stiff, hot, and stifling.

So why do I long for one now? It has occurred to me, all these years later, as I garden with greasy sunblock slathered all over my face and neck and a white handkerchief and old cap with a big visor over my head, that a sunbonnet would be just perfect to keep me sheltered from the sun as it did when I was a girl. I might even look a bit less like a scarecrow as I weed my flower beds.

Sunbonnets and mamas. Treasures we don't fully appreciate until we don't have them any longer.

Marilyn Kratz has had about 500 stories, articles and poems published, mostly for children. Her fourth book, a nonfiction picture book, will be out in 2011. "I Wish I had my Sunbonnet" was originally published in *The Fence Post*, Ogallala, Nebraska, in 2006.

INGENUITY

Marie Wells

In the early nineteen thirties, the Great Depression hovered over America like an enormous predator. Our family felt its talons when Dad was foreclosed on and sold out on a farm near Dickens, Iowa in 1931. We moved to another farm west of Milford in February. Farmers and their families needed a great deal of ingenuity to survive those years.

"Mom, will I get to go to school?" I asked anxiously soon after we moved.

Mother nodded. "I talked to the teacher today," she replied. I was overjoyed. Though I'd turned five the previous fall, my parents had thought I was too small to go.

I loved walking the mile to country school with three brothers carrying syrup pails that held our lunches. I loved learning, and I loved recess. In April, a favorite pastime of my schoolmates was shooting marbles. Glen and Dale, two older brothers, had a few battered glass ones, but Orville and I had none.

One Saturday my brother Orville said, "Go inside and get some water. We'll make our own marbles."

I ran into the house, pumped water from the small cistern pump into a tin can and carried it carefully outdoors. Orville poured it over some hard clay that surrounded the foundation of the house. We dug up pieces of clay like two squirrels digging for nuts and rolled them into half-inch balls, dried them in the sunshine until they were hard and happily played with them.

Sometimes we played house with our kittens dressed in doll clothes as our children. Even we little kids used ingenuity to entertain ourselves, as we had few toys.

Late one afternoon, Mother called, "Orville, Marie, come gather the eggs."

Reluctantly, we left our play, grabbed the pan and poked into dips and hollows in the grove for hidden "henfruit." In the henhouse, Orville yanked a cross old Leghorn hen off her nest to get hers, while I searched the henless nests. Outside, with two dozen eggs in tow, we paraded toward the house. My brother spied a scruffy old broom propped against the cobhouse.

"Get that broom," Orville said.

"Why?" I asked.

"Just get it," he ordered.

When I did, he handed me the pan, grabbed the broom by the handle holding it horizontally about two feet off the ground and told me to set the pan on the sweeping end.

I did. After a few steps, the broom tipped.

Eggsaster struck!

The pan crashed to the ground resulting in dirty, yellow smashed eggs. With trepidation, we scooped the filthy mess into the pan and slunk with telltale hands into the kitchen. Mother was not pleased. She didn't spank us. She never spanked. But with a few sharp words, she let us know that she was ashamed of us. That was even worse!

In those times, eggs were a priceless commodity for our family. Our weekly crate of twelve dozen eggs brought less than a dollar in trade for groceries at a Milford store. If mother got a few cents back in cash, she would walk blocks on painful, swollen feet to the other two grocery stores to save a few pennies. The two-dozen smashed eggs would have provided enough money to buy fresh fruit for our five school lunches for a week.

Mother used a lot of ingenuity when combining her few purchases with her home canned produce. She always made delicious and nutritious meals for her family of eight.

My sister, Mildred, used her ingenuity when designing, sewing and remodeling clothes for us. She sewed all of her own and my school clothes and remodeled some of mother's

Our parents managed to eke out a living in 1931 because the rent was low. They hoped for a better year in 1932. Little did they know!

In the spring, Dick, our big blind workhorse, caught his foot in a barbed wire fence one night. By morning he had sawed his hoof halfway off. Dad had to destroy him, leaving him short a team. Dick's death was a great loss.

Catastrophe struck on a torrid day in late July when Dad collapsed in a neighbor's barnyard while pitching bundles into a threshing machine. One neighbor thought he had died when he turned cold and grey. Then another noticed him breathing. The two of them gently placed him in the back seat of the car, drove him home and laid him on his bed. Mother frantically called Dr. Buchanan, who drove the eight miles to our house.

"He has heat exhaustion," explained the doctor. He ordered Dad to stay in bed for a week and not get too tired or overheated ever again. We kids had to be whisper-quiet so Dad could rest.

Dad did gradually get stronger. In the meantime, my brother Howard, who had just graduated from high school, had the responsibility of taking over the farm work.

Summer drifted into fall and misfortune hit again. Dad's ancient Samson tractor wouldn't run after we moved. Dad allowed Dale and Glen to tinker with it. Eventually, they got it started. That was a real plus after losing Dick. But during fall plowing, a connecting rod in the motor of the Samson broke loose and rammed a hole in the oil pan, resulting in the loss of all the oil.

"Can't be fixed," stated our neighbor, John Erickson. "It's cast iron. Can't be welded."

Howard hated driving plodding horses. He had a passion for machines, experimenting with engines and repairing them whenever he could. With patience, he studied the break. With Dad's help, he stretched a piece of inner-tube across the hole and secured it with pieces of board and some bolts. It re-established the oil pressure. He replaced the connecting rod and the oil, and finished the fall work with alacrity. Howard's ingenuity was remarkable.

Icy blasts heralded the winter. It was so frigid that the drinking water in the kitchen pail froze at night. Since the log fire in the small metal stove in the living room, our only source of heat, was allowed to die down at bedtime, the temperature would be glacial in the morning. Often I thought that I wouldn't get warm until spring.

When dead trees became scarce and coal too costly, Dad decided to burn his eight-cent-a bushel corn for fuel. He built a cart from discarded wheels with an axle, and added a framework, a deck and a handle. My brothers used it to haul bushel baskets of ear corn to the house. The corn produced a hot, steady heat. We were warmer in the evenings thanks to dad's ingenuity.

The final calamity of the year occurred in December when our 1920 Dodge car broke down beyond repair. Despair set in because at Christmastime the entire family would need transportation. Christmas at our grandma's homes was thirty miles away. The only movie we saw all year was the free one sponsored by the Milford merchants. Although we couldn't afford a tree, we could enjoy the beautiful one at church where I was supposed to be in the program.

Christmas at our house would consist of a few decorations and a small wrapped gift beside each plate at breakfast time— but we were thrilled! Even our parents would receive a gift this year from us four younger kids. Dale had begged a nickel from mother and bought them two cookie cutters.

Howard thought that he might have a solution to our transportation problem. He owned a 1916 four-cylinder Dodge truck that he had earned working for a neighbor.

"It's the fastest four in America," he declared.

He stripped parts from an abandoned digging machine left by the west side of the farm. Diligently, he constructed a hoist in the alleyway of the granary and attached it to the beams above. After pushing the old Dodge into the alleyway, he detached the body from the frame and hoisted the car body up high. When the boys had pushed the car frame outside, he backed his truck in and carefully lowered the car body down into the grain box.

"There she is!" he exclaimed triumphantly.

Thereafter, when the family needed to travel, all the Taylor kids, except me, scrambled into the car body, which was inside the truck box. I was told to ride in the cab. The others cocooned themselves in blankets and robes because there was no heat back there.

Even the Spencer paper carried a picture of the contraption.

My sister Mildred was highly humiliated to think that her high school friends would learn that we were so poor. However, Howard's ingenuity saved Christmas and supplied transportation for us for several months.

When Franklin Roosevelt became president in 1933, conditions gradually improved. Dad was able to purchase a 1928 Dodge Victory, which cheered all of us immensely.

Eventually Dad was able to buy the land that he had farmed for so long. But in those spare years during the Great Depression, the ingenuity shown by every member of the family served all of us well.

Marie Wells has lived in Marathon, Iowa, for 51 years in a home that's been in the Wells family for 111 years. She enjoys writing about her childhood on a farm near Milford, Iowa, so that present and future generations will know how life was lived back then.

Photo provided by Debi Iske

FINDING MY HEART IN THE HEARTLAND

Jean Tennant

When people first learn that I grew up in San Diego and moved to Iowa while a junior in high school, their questions are always the same: How did I get here, and why did I stay?

The answer to the first question is a little complicated. My stepfather, who was from rural Iowa, moved to California to seek his fortune in the big city, where he met and married my mother, a divorcee with three children. Then, tired of the city after a few years, he wanted to return to Iowa to re-enter the family business, and my mother agreed. This was in the early seventies and at the time I was a rebellious teen enthusiastically embracing the post-hippy culture of my home state. I'm quite sure that if we'd stayed I would now have children with names like Sunshine, Moonbeam and Wildflower.

The answer to the second question is easier. I've stayed because I found, after the initial shock wore off and I'd become accustomed to the smell of cow manure, that I like it here. The land is flat and the wind blows incessantly, but the people are friendly, and they stubbornly refuse to give in to the urban cynicism I'd previously known. I went from a ninth grade class of more than 600 students to a graduating class of 26. I was one of just fourteen girls. Adding to the culture shock, we moved into a farmhouse—rented for $50 a month— where, without a driver's license, I was a virtual prisoner amongst the corn fields. But we had a horse, a dog and a dozen or so barn cats that I loved.

In junior high I'd thought nothing of hopping a city bus for a ride to the famous zoo, or, better yet, the beach. On the farm I had to beg a ride to town, only to find there wasn't much going on there anyway.

I also found a warmth here I'd never quite experienced before. By the time I graduated from high school I was no longer plotting my return to California. I was content to further my education nearby, and by the time I had children of my own I'd learned the value of small town living in keeping them, for the most part, out of harm's way.

That's not to say I didn't give city life the occasional try. We lived in Minneapolis for a couple of years, but the cost of living was high and the traffic scary. I came back in part because, after a divorce, I couldn't afford to live there on my own. In Iowa, I was able to buy a three-bedroom ranch style house on a double lot for about $60,000, and I don't often bother to lock the doors (though I probably will after this).

Shortly after we moved back, my middle child came home one day and said, "Some lady uptown said 'Hi, Paul' to me. I don't know who she was. How does she know me?"

"Everybody here knows who you are," I told him. "Get used to it."

It keeps us all on our best behavior.

A couple of years ago I left my billfold on the trunk of my car after filling the tank with gas. I didn't miss it until hours later, when there was a knock at my door. A tall, bearded man held out my battered billfold.

"I was behind you and saw it bounce off your car onto the road," he explained. "When it hit the ground it burst open and everything scattered. I think I found most of it, but there might be some change missing." My wallet was stuffed with credit cards, my driver's license, about $60 in cash and assorted coupons and store receipts. This kind soul had dodged oncoming traffic to chase it all down—fluttering, I'm sure, in the breeze of passing cars—and return it to me.

There are a few concessions I haven't made. I'm still a seafood-and-wild rice person in a meat-and-potatoes community, and I recently paid $125 for second-day air delivery of $75 worth of the Portuguese linguica sausage that I love but can't get around here. But the occasional sense of isolation I might feel has been put to rest by the advent of the Internet, a true godsend for those of us who choose to live in the boonies. Shopping, which was once a problem, is now just a mouse-click away, and I maintain a close personal relationship with Amazon.com.

For me, there's no going back. The new shingles on my roof are John Deere green, and the Midwest is so thoroughly in my blood that if I cut myself cornmeal would flow from my veins.

The best part, however, is that Sunshine, Moonbeam and Wildflower are named Shaun, Paul and Toni.

Jean Tennant grew up in San Diego, California, and moved to small-town Iowa when she was in high school. Her books have been published by Silhouette, Kensington, and Warner. For the past several years she has taught writing throughout the Midwest, for which her schedule can be seen at www.JeanTennant.com.

CITY GIRL VIEW

Rebecca Groff

As a young girl, I didn't know about things like mastitis in milk cows, or trichinosis worries in pigs—except what they taught us about it in health class at school. I didn't realize that the loss of even one milk cow could leave worry lines as deep as the Grand Canyon in the forehead of a dairy farmer who was trying to build up his herd, enabling him to support his family.

Technically, I was raised a city girl—if you're willing to call a rural Iowa farming community whose population never exceeded one thousand—a "city." And while I never actually lived on a farm with hip-roofed red barns, and hay wagons hitched to Allis Chalmers tractors parked alongside tin machine sheds, my early life was literally framed by the influence of the farming lifestyle.

My husband describes farming in five short words: A lot of hard work.

His memories of the farming life include hand shoveling feed from morning 'til night for several hundred head of cattle in the bitter cold during wicked Iowa blizzards when the power went out, and keeping the ice broken out of the watering tanks so the animals could drink. His family didn't have a power generator on the farm, and without power the automatic feeders were useless.

He told me he'd wanted to play baseball with his friends in town during the summers but his skills were needed instead on his family's farm for summer field work, painting barns or baling hay. He remembers stacking bales inside a suffocating hayloft where the prickly, loose particulate-dust of cut hay clung to sweaty skin and tormented nasal passages in hot, muggy conditions typical of blistering Iowa summers.

These aren't exactly fond memories for him. And even though the sweet purple scent of cut clover remains one of his favorite smells today, along with a reverent partiality for the pictorial architecture of the rural Iowa landscape, I also know that he didn't look back once when he left for his new life on the Iowa State University campus in 1969.

My family and I lived on a triple-sized lot at the edge of town right where the paving in front of our house turned to gravel. We called this dusty road Cemetery Road because if you followed it out of town, it carried you to the cemetery. A cornfield lined the south side of our property with the remnants of a couple of small farms flanking the field's backside. The railroad tracks were just beyond those.

Just east of our place was a low-lying vacant lot where one of the local implement dealers stored excess tractors, combines and manure spreaders. We kids used to climb around that equipment in the summer, often playing hide and seek among all of the interesting iron configurations. In the winter we went sledding down the steep decline of the pathway they used to access the rows of equipment.

So while I didn't live on a farm, I was closer to the spacious flavor of a farm setting than most of my townie friends. Add to that the fact that over half of my classmates in school were farmers' kids. Many of their dads were frequent and loyal customers of my dad, who was possibly their best business partner in town, as he operated the welding/blacksmith repair shop.

Not only did I have all the essence of country living from this location, but the substance, too, from the farming stories that Dad brought home at night, in addition to the tales and experiences my friends would share at school.

In the summer the strong feedlot tang of a cattle feeding operation south of town wound its way through our window screens, and in the early mornings I awakened to the crowing roosters kept by the lady who lived down near the train tracks. These ambiances of country life were as natural to my day as they were to any farm kid.

I witnessed the aftermath of a hog slaughter on the farm place that belonged to the bachelor brothers of a woman named Norma. She occasionally helped my mother with cleaning and babysitting. One afternoon Norma needed to retrieve something from her brothers' house so she took me along. We heard their commotion coming from down by the big barn so went to see what was up. Hanging from the barn's peak, swinging on a sturdy cable, was the headless corpse of a hog. They must have just hoisted it as it was still swaying between them.

One of them gave it a playful final slap before pushing it again. They were laughing and seemed to be having fun. The other brother caught it on the return swing and began rinsing it down with water cupped in his hands. His pats seemed almost affectionate as rivulets of pale pink bloody water dripped on the ground.

Inherently, I knew where meat, milk and eggs came from. I just wasn't sure why they were enjoying themselves so. But I guess I did what most of us do—I blanked out the in-between from barn to dinner table. But I've never forgotten that shiny wet pig swinging so casually in the bright sunlight that day.

I also accompanied Norma when she had baby lambs to feed. I'd watch as she filled a large milk bottle with water, stirring in some dry powder that made it look like really thin milk, slip on a huge nipple and secure it.

She let me help one time. "Now hold on tight or else they'll pull it right out of your hands," she instructed. It was magical to watch them suck and I couldn't believe the way they attacked that nipple, emptying the tall bottle in what seemed like a matter of seconds.

"Can we give them another bottle?" I asked.

"No. They only get one for now," she explained.

Their small faces looked like black velvet and occasionally I could get one quick touch in before they'd back away from the wood fence.

The reality of the life of a chicken came to me on the cement slab behind our house. My dad came home from work one night carrying a gunny sack with several crabby, bobbing chickens boxing their way around inside. Who would ever want to be stuffed inside one of those oily-smelling bags? Dad pulled one out by its feet, using his foot to hold it down long enough to get the dirty deed with the axe accomplished.

As he raised the axe he gave me a quick, grim look as if to say, "It's gotta be done—"

I knew what was coming, but I also knew I didn't need to watch. I chose instead to go down to our basement kitchen where my mother and one of her farmwife friends were doing the next part.

The air in the kitchen was heavy with steam, and all of the smallish basement windows coated with condensation from the pots of hot, bloody water on the stove. Hot, bloody chicken water is not a smell easily forgotten. It reminded me of the strong rusty red taste in my mouth after the dentist finished pulling a tooth. There were feathers all over the gray cement floor and piles of mauve-pink innards piling up on sheets of newspapers as my mother and her friend worked steadily to remove every last pin feather from the naked chicken bodies. And yet, in spite of those vivid scenes, the duplicitous fact is that fried chicken was my favorite, and my mother fried a chicken worthy of the gods.

My earliest childhood fears of large livestock probably came about from a visit to the dairy farm owned by a good family friend.

"Do you want to walk out to the milking parlor?" they asked me. I nodded yes, of course. I loved any opportunity to visit someone's farm. It fascinated me to see farmyards filled with roaming, pecking chickens, and kittens of every color running and chasing around a weathered picnic table or hiding underneath the vehicles parked in the yard as flies buzzed around their feeding dishes, landing and creating a dirty-looking feel. It all was the most exotic sense of freedom for a city kid.

Their milking barn had that muted warmed-milk smell that mixed in with my excitement, and made me feel nauseous. What they forgot to tell me, however, was that once they finished milking those giants, they released the cows from their stanchions, and that those cows would be eager to get back outside. So suddenly, when I realized the cows were now loose, I pasted myself against the wall of the barn in fear that they were coming to bite me, or run me down with their massive black and white bodies. Those big heads with their large liquid brown eyes watched me widely as they moved out. I'm not sure who was more bothered—them or me. Most likely, it was me.

Back inside their house we all sat down to thick chocolate cake—and milk, of course. The family had a machine on their kitchen counter that separated the cream from the milk and pasteurized it for their drinking needs. Everyone was sitting around the oilcloth covered kitchen table ready to enjoy their own piece of cake when someone set a glass of milk in front of me. I took a sip. It was the worst glass of milk I'd ever tasted. Our milk at home was icy cold. This stuff was warm and thick-tasting. My opposition to its qualities was observed and forgiven. But my piece of chocolate cake disappeared without argument—or milk.

I recently commented to a former high school chum—a farm kid herself—that I thought I would've enjoyed growing up on a farm. She quickly reminded me that anything sounds good in theory.

It's true that I never drove a tractor or put up hay, and I never helped castrate pigs or shovel out hog houses. But as a city girl exposed to the farm life activities and flavors that went on around me daily, I acquired my own set of memories about a few of the joys as well as the realities of the agrarian way of life. And to this day, I've no desire to be without any of them.

Rebecca Groff lives in Cedar Rapids where she does freelance writing for area newspapers and magazines. She leads a monthly writing class at the Cedar Rapids Museum of History and launched her new blog in the summer of 2010. http://rebeccasnotepad.wordpress.com.

Photo provided by Karen J. Schutt

THE SINGING SILO

Karen J. Schutt

All my morning chores were finished. I'd made my bed, dried and put away the breakfast dishes, and brought in two pails of corncobs for the cook stove. Together my sister Marilyn and I had picked a pail of green beans and pulled an armful of rhubarb stalks. So I was free until time to set the table for dinner.

I skipped off to play in the grove but made a detour through the empty cattle lots. The cattle were in the pasture so I could safely explore. A tall empty silo stood between the two lots waiting for corn chopping that was months away. Against the silo was a little silage house that was the right size for a playhouse. But Dad told me not to fill it with my playhouse junk because I would just have to haul it away before the harvest. I didn't really want to make a playhouse there anyway because of the wasps. They made little mud nests up near the roof and didn't like to be disturbed. If a wasp was disturbed it would sting you. They weren't friendly at all.

I had a bad run-in with wasps a while back. I was jumping on the platform of the old binder and the wasps living there didn't like that. They flew up and around, angry as could be. So I borrowed the spray gun from the milking parlor and sprayed them. They flew faster than I could run and my arm and shoulder were stung. I ran shrieking to the house just as Dad was about to start the milking.

He said I would probably live and asked if I had learned a lesson. Then he told me to go back and get the spray gun. I tiptoed up to the binder, fearfully watching for the wasps, grabbed the gun and hustled back to the barn. Dad also told me to leave the spray gun alone after this; that the fly spray was poisonous. But my shoulder and arm hurt for quite a while even after Mom put baking soda on them.

There didn't seem to be any new wasp nests, so it was safe

to explore the silage house. Inside, a person could look up the chute to the top of the silo. This was where, in winter, Dad threw down forkfuls of silage that collected in the little house. Then he would carry it forkful by forkful down the line of feed bunks for the cattle to eat. Little square doors went all the way up to the top inside the chute. The doors were removed to throw down the silage and replaced when the level inside the silo went down.

There were a few of the lower doors stacked on the floor. I lay back on the pile and pushed until my head was inside the silo, through the lowest opening. I looked up and watched the clouds float by. This was fun until my neck started to hurt.

I rolled over onto my stomach and looked at the bottom of the silo. It looked swampy and slimy and dangerous. If you fell in maybe you would sink out of sight and never be seen again.

The thought of that made me shiver.

But the silo was a wonderful place for echoes. I shouted, "HEY!" as loudly as I could. It echoed and re-echoed in a very satisfying way.

I thought of hollering some of my family's names: "DAD! MOM! MARILYN! GRANDMA! BARBIE! UNCLE DAN!"

What a racket!

I decided to sing a song. The song that came to my mind was: "HOOOME, HOOOME, ON THE RAAANGE."

That sounded wonderful!

Then at the top of my lungs I sang: "JEEESUS LOVES MEEE THIS I KNOOOW!"

Then: "ROW, ROW, ROW YOUR BOAT, GENTLY DOWN THE STREEEEAM, MARILYN, MARILYN, MARILYN, MARILYN, LIFE IS BUT A DREEEEAM."

Then: "AWAAAY IN A MAAANGER, NOOO CRIB FOR A BED."

After singing all the songs I could remember, I was out of breath and thirsty so I headed back to the house for a drink of water. It also might be time to set the table for dinner. I was good about remembering that job. The time to do that was when the short hand was on eleven and the long hand was on twelve.

When I got to the house Mom said I should wash my hands and set the table even though it was early. "And set another place because Robert will be here. He's using your dad's tools to fix his cultivator, so I told him he might as well stay for dinner. Heaven knows what there is to eat at his house."

Robert was our bachelor neighbor who lived across the section. I didn't know if I liked that Robert would be here because he teased me all the time, and I never knew how to react. Usually his teasing just made me mad.

But I carefully set five places: Mom on one side, then Dad on the next, Robert on the third side, and Marilyn and I sat around the corner.

At twelve o'clock the beans, meat, potatoes and gravy were on the table. Dad was in from the field and everyone was washed and combed, and ready to eat. Marilyn and I sat with our hands on our laps until the food was passed to us.

Robert thought he would hold the bowl of beans for me to help myself, but I firmly took it away from him and set it between my place and Marilyn's. I did not want Robert to help me, ever. He just grinned.

Everyone was eating and talking and minding their manners when Robert said, "Someone must have had their radio turned up real loud this morning."

"Really?" said Mom, as she refilled the coffee cups.

"Yeah, I was hearing all kinds of singing. Sounded like it came from over by the silo, but I don't know how that could be."

"I don't know either," said Mom. "It certainly wasn't our radio, ours wasn't even turned on."

Marilyn gave me a sideways look but didn't say anything. I could feel my ears getting hot and I slid down in my chair. I wouldn't look at Robert. He never teased Marilyn.

"Yeah, it was quite a concert," said Robert.

"Well, my goodness," said Mom.

"Sit up, Karen," said Dad.

I was glad when they started talking about other things. As soon as I finished my rhubarb cobbler, I excused myself. I went out to the swing and sat, drawing circles in the dirt with my big toe and feeling sorry for myself. I hadn't known my singing would carry all the way to the machine shed, but then I hadn't known Robert would be there, either.

After a while Mom called me to help clear the table and dry the dishes. As I rounded the corner of the house I saw Dad and Robert sitting on the porch, visiting before going back to their work.

As I passed Robert he said, "Yep, it was quite a concert."

I stomped into the house and slammed the screen door. I could hear both of them laughing. Mom said I shouldn't let a little thing like that bother me, and don't slam doors, but I still felt hot and angry.

A few evenings later Robert drove into the yard in his rackety pickup truck. After a bit Dad called, "Karen! Come here! Robert wants to see you."

Reluctantly I went out on the porch where they were sitting. Robert had both hands behind his back. "Got something for you. Guess which hand."

I eyed him suspiciously.

"Well, guess which hand," he repeated.

I chose his right hand. "Nope, not the right one."

Then I heard a loud meow. "That one!" I pointed to his left hand.

From behind his back Robert brought a kitten, quite small, black with four white paws, white chest, and a white tip on its tail. He put it in my hands.

"Boots said he would rather live with you than with a mean old bachelor like me."

I cuddled Boots to my cheek and listened to him purr.

"What do you say?" asked Dad.

"Oh, thank you, Robert!"

From then on Robert and I were friends. Sort of.

Karen J. Schutt lives near Sioux Falls, South Dakota, with her husband Charles and cat Butch. Besides family, her interests include traveling, quilting, and writing, but not singing.

A Poem About My Pet

BOOTS

By Karen J.
Age 7

Boots is my cat
He is big and fat.

He is black and white,
And can see in the night.

He has soft fur
I love to hear him purr.

He is my friend.
The end.

Photo provided by Mary Berdan

CURLY HAIR

Mary Berdan

As a child, everyone I met commented on my naturally curly hair. "It's beautiful!" they would say.

I hated it.

My mother always kept my hair cut quite short, in a "pixie" style of the day. Many of my friends had long hair that they wore in ponytails or braids. They even wore brightly colored ribbons or bows that coordinated with their clothes. I was envious.

After my mother died, my father, who liked long hair, allowed me to grow my hair out. It was an exciting experience for me.

The school year following my mother's death, I was in the third grade and my black hair had grown to just past my jaw line. When it was time for school pictures, I couldn't have been more excited because I now had long hair!

My dear, inexperienced father tried his best to deal with a young daughter and agreed to help me curl my hair for my school picture the following day. The "flip" hairstyle was the fad at the time for girls.

So, to the store we went to buy pink foam rollers to curl my hair. My father and I dampened my long hair the night before my school pictures and carefully parted it into sections and gently rolled each section upward in the pink rollers for me to sleep on all night as my hair dried.

It would be "flipped" in the morning. I was so excited, and just knew I would be beautiful.

Morning came and Dad woke me up for school. I could hardly wait to take the rollers out of my hair. Gently, so as not to pull my hair, Dad and I unrolled my long locks.

A little brushing . . . and then tears!

The right side was curled up much shorter than the left. How could I go to school and have my picture taken when I looked so awful, so *uneven*?

Dad brushed and brushed the shorter side of curls, while trying to console his nine-year-old daughter and make it all better. Eventually some of the curl relaxed, but I was still unhappy. I had been looking forward to this being my best school picture yet with my new hairstyle. It wasn't turning out that way.

My father tucked a hairbrush in my school bag for me to take to school, along with a note to my teacher explaining the events that had led to this disaster. The note asked that she try to tame the shorter, curlier side prior to pictures.

My teacher did her best. She worked on my hair and tried hard to settle my anxiety, but I still wasn't totally convinced that my pictures would turn out okay.

When the school pictures finally came back, though, it was hardly noticeable that one side of my hair was a wee bit shorter than the other. And by then it didn't matter—I had long hair for the first time in my life and I was beautiful!

Mary Berdan has lived in Sleepy Eye, Minnesota, for 30 years. She and her husband have three children, two daughters already "out of the nest" and a son who will be a high school senior. They are happy to have raised their children in a small town.

LITTLE RED STOMPING HOOD

Keith Jensen

If one were familiar with southeast South Dakota and carefully placed one's thumb over a certain area on a decent-sized South Dakota map, one could pretty much cover that area known as Little Denmark.

In that area, there were a number of churches, lots of country schools, and a couple of country towns. In 1941, my family and I lived on a farm towards the southern part of Little Denmark. Our lives revolved around two institutions a mile apart. Both played a huge part in our lives, and though they were very different they were very much alike.

Our one-room schoolhouse fit in well with the sparseness of the prairie. The building itself was quite small, with no basement, just a small room for coats and overshoes, and a classroom, but it was larger than the other building on the one-acre lot—the outhouse. A coal stove provided the heat, and a piece of tin surrounded the stove for a purpose I never did figure out. A teacher's desk, 20 student desks, and a piano sat inside the room.

The church was in the style of the other country churches, with white siding, a very tall bell tower, a generous entry, beautiful windows, the worship area, and a balcony. The basement held a generous number of people for wedding receptions, silver and golden wedding parties, special church festivals, and funerals. The cemetery surrounded the church on three sides, and the outbuilding was behind the church, so the Christians could maintain a fair amount of modesty when nature made the visit necessary.

The school was open eight months of the year to fit the rhythm of the farm families. All of our classmates had last names ending in "sen": Christensen, Sorensen, Swensen, Larsen, Jensen.

Many of the same families attended the church but other Danish families brought new names like Storgaard, Tanderuup, and Fastruup. Still, we were 100 percent Danish.

The big event each year at school was the Christmas program. Country school teachers knew that their competence was often determined by the quality of the program, so they seemed to take an inordinate amount of time during school days to practice for the program. We students practiced speaking clearly and loudly, working out every detail to perfection. The program had to be faultless.

The fathers came in several weeks in advance of the program to build a small stage at the front of the room. Wires were strung and sheets were hung so the main stage would have curtains that opened and closed, just like on Broadway. The girls had a private area stage left, and the boys shared their privacy with the coal stove on stage right.

On the night of the performance, the student desks were pushed to the east and west sides where the little brothers and sisters could sit, along with friends and cousins. The mothers sat in the middle and the fathers stood in the back. With the room packed and the windows decorated, the dim lantern that hung from the ceiling helped hide the bareness of the room.

The Second World War was in full swing so it wasn't a surprise that our teacher had picked out plays dealing with the war, and war songs were sung to honor the neighbor boys who were in the military.

My brother, four years older than I, got the idea that the play would be more realistic if he used his rhythm-band stick to strike the tin surrounding the stove to make it sound like bombs were falling. He was so impressed with the results that the "bombs" began to fall faster and louder. Once the teacher figured out who was making the racket, she made an emergency dash to stage left to end the sound effects. This she did with a simple thumb-tap to his head, which immediately ended the noisiest bomb attack of World War II.

She was also unimpressed when he chose to deliver the punch line of the play in Danish, but it was too late to remedy that piece of creativity. And, after all, she was protecting her credentials for future employment.

The church Christmas program was directed by the Sunday school teachers, the mothers of the church. The programs were historical in nature and it was predictable that some of the younger students would make errors and have memory lapses that added to the charm of the program.

The congregation never got tired of seeing this year's Mary rocking the baby Jesus, while Joseph in his father's bathrobe stood watch. Shepherds, wise men, and angels appeared to tell the glorious story.

Our church was the most beautiful building I had ever seen, especially the interior, on Christmas night. The altar consisted of many spires pointing to heaven itself, while a beautiful, life-sized statue of Christ stood in the middle. The high ceilings created little corners of blackness, and lamps that stood on beautiful sconces lit up arched windows with frosted lacy panes and squares of colored glass. The Christmas tree was just inside the communion railing, and on the other side of the room stood the pulpit, which the pastor entered by climbing five steps. The pump organ moaned ethereal notes clear up to the balcony. The pews easily held the Christmas guests.

But something entirely unexpected happened toward the end of the program. The parishioners were farm families with the exception of one family from town who had a girl who was Sunday school age. Because the family found it difficult to travel the distance, their church attendance was irregular and we children were unfamiliar with this little girl who was listed on the program as singing a solo.

It was with some curiosity that we watched her come forward for her part in the program. Then something happened toward the middle of the solo that irritated this little red haired girl. She stomped her foot, pointed her finger at us and declare in a loud voice, "I won't, I won't, I won't sing one more word!" And she stomped back to sit by her mother.

I was bewildered as to what prompted her behavior. Most likely there was some rib poking and giggling among the shepherds and Joseph, but since I was one of the wise men, I knew enough not to participate in making the little red-headed girl uncomfortable.

Our teachers accused us of behaving badly, which had caused this little spitfire to assume we were making fun of her. Nevertheless, we received our favorite Christmas treat of the year, a brown sack with an apple and an orange, some ribbon candy, and lots of peanuts in the shell.

But I was smitten and this little whippersnapper became my wife thirteen years later.

Keith Jensen was an educator for 43 years in the upper Midwest and for the National Education Association. He and "Little Red" live in The Lodge, Sioux Falls, South Dakota. Keith continues to find magic in words and marvels at the wonderful images they create.

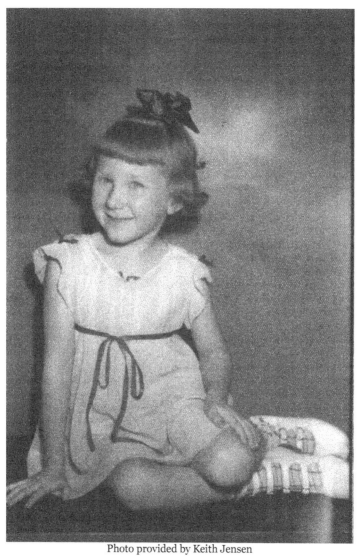

Photo provided by Keith Jensen

Photo provided by Ruth Hunziker Underhill

LOVE OF WORDS BEGAN IN A SINGLE ROOM

Ruth Hunziker Underhill

One of the fondest memories that has been forever etched in my mind and engraved in my heart is that of the little one-room schoolhouse that six of my siblings and I attended, and which housed all eight grades.

Cottonwood School was nestled among tall trees in the country, about five miles northeast of the small town of Washington, Illinois. Our farm was located about a mile due east of the school, which today is on Cruger Road.

The school building was very small, only able to contain ten to twelve desks at most. The teacher had to arrive at the school an hour ahead of the students in the winter because, along with teaching, it was her duty to fire up the old potbellied stove in the rear of the school room so it would be warm when the students arrived. At that time, there were very few men in the teaching profession.

Each morning we always opened the school day by saying the "Pledge of Allegiance" with our hands over our hearts. The Bible was *always* displayed on the teacher's desk. Some mornings the teacher would begin the day by reading a chapter from some educational or exciting nonfiction book. Often we could hardly wait for the next day to hear the next chapter. It kept us in eager anticipation.

The teacher's desk was in the front of the tiny room, and about six feet in front of her desk was a "recitation bench." When it was time for each grade's classes (whether it was readin', writin' or 'rithmetic,) that grade was called up to the front to take their place on the "recitation bench." There the teacher diligently taught each subject for each class, one by one, throughout the day.

While each grade's class was in session on the bench, the remainder of students were expected to quietly continue studying their lessons, blocking out what was taking place in the front of the room. I don't recall that we had difficulty concentrating while another class was reciting up front. I also don't recall having the mountains of homework that is required of children today. We seemed to have ample time to do our school work during the regular school hours. And even though we weren't taught much beyond the basics, Cottonwood School produced some pretty successful people and we learned to get along socially without counselors.

I'll never forget my first day of school. Every morning, when my two older brothers and two older sisters left for school, my younger sister and I would sit on the front steps and cry because we couldn't go with them. But finally I turned five (there was no kindergarten, first grade began at age five) and it was my turn to go to school!

I still remember how eager I was and exactly what I wore that day. Carefully I put on the crisply-ironed, little red print dress with tiny white stars all over it. My oldest brother, who was in eighth grade, took me on his bicycle. My heart pounded with excitement as we started out the door and neared the school. I was five years old and had been waiting for this day forever!

When the teacher took down all the vital student information (they didn't pre-register as they do today . . . you just showed up), lo and behold, she candidly announced, to my dismay, that she didn't know how to teach first grade, and I was sent back home to wait yet another year!

The tears were back, as that was one of the most devastating experiences of my life. I'd have to wait another lifetime to start school.

The following year, when I finally got to officially attend school, recess and lunchtime were the two most enjoyable events that we eagerly anticipated each day. At recess we played many group games (as many as eight to ten people could play at a time) such as dare base, hide-and-seek, handy-over, kick-the-can, etc.

There was a small shed filled with corncobs used to start the heating stove in the winter. Many times, in nice weather, we would retreat to that little shed and sit on top of the corncobs to eat our lunch. Our lunch often consisted of a sandwich (many times smashed navy beans, with catsup), fruit, cookies and lip-smacking homemade chocolate pudding that Mom had cooked early that morning, put in a little glass container and poured fresh cream on top. With loving hands, Mom packed six lunches every morning having, at times, very little to work with. She always saved the outside bread wrappers to use for our sandwiches. There was no such thing as sandwich bags and we couldn't afford waxed paper.

Most of the students in the school were just my siblings, our cousins and myself. School buses were unheard of. Our mode of transportation was walking, riding a bicycle or, in our case, riding in our rickety little pony cart pulled by our faithful little pony, Billy. There was even a small pony shed at the school to protect Billy from the weather while we were in school.

One day, a strange thing happened. Somehow Billy loosened his reins and escaped. When we were ready to leave school, we had to unite our efforts and pull the pony cart home ourselves. Upon our arrival, Billy was waiting in the barnyard to greet us with loving licks, as if to say, "Where've you been?"

When I was in the fourth grade, there were only three students in the entire school—my two sisters and myself. What a deal! We didn't have to be there until 10:00 a.m. and got out at 1:30 p.m.

The following year our beloved little Cottonwood School closed, and we three sisters were shipped off to another one-room school about three miles away, where there were lots and lots of other kids. At least 15!

Even though that little school has long been closed, it's been an open page inscribed in my mind for all these years. It has been moved and now sits at the very south edge of the little town of Washington, Illinois, and is being used as a home.

As you drive by, you can still see the imprint of where the name "Cottonwood School" was tacked on the front of the little dollhouse building, and is a treasured reminder of the joys of childhood. When I drive by it, I feel almost as though I'm treading on sacred ground.

I have written many published works of poetry through the past 70 years, and my love for words all began in my formative years at Cottonwood School. What a lingering, treasured memory to hold in one's heart and mind throughout a lifetime!

COTTONWOOD SCHOOL

Back in a grove of cottonwood trees
Stood a tiny country school.
There in a little shady nook
We learned the golden rule.

Not many children in those days
Eight grades all in one room,
But we learned to play together
And we kept our hearts in tune.

We studied hard, hour by hour
Till recess came along.
Then out we'd dash to the grassy yard.
My what a happy throng.

One day we built a tree house
In a cottonwood tree up high.
We could hardly wait till lunch time
To eat our sack lunch in the sky!

-Ruth Hunziker Underhill

Ruth Hunziker Underhill was born in 1933 into a family with seven siblings. Times were tough for their parents in her growing-up years, but they had lots of love and manufactured their own simple entertainment. In April 2010 she and her husband Stephen celebrated their 57th wedding anniversary. She has been intrigued with words ever since she was old enough to read and write, whether it be writing or playing word games.

THE BUS

Leslie Means

His name was Jim Corner. But to many of the kids who rode his long bus route, he was simply known as "The Scary Bus Driver."

He had a look that could cut through your body, a stern voice that gave chills and even worse, eyes in the back of his head. I tell you this not as a fictional Halloween story, but from the true-life perspective of a young child.

I lived only seven miles from town. That wasn't far, considering the distance some of my classmates had to travel, but for some reason I had the longest bus route. I was either the first kid picked up in the morning and the first to be dropped off in the afternoon, or the last to be picked up and the last to be dropped off. All in all, the trip was well over an hour.

We switched every semester, but to me, both scenarios were a lose-lose situation.

It started in first grade. I remember being so excited to ride that big yellow bus for the first time. I had watched my older sisters get on and off that huge machine every day and I'd anxiously awaited my turn. Obviously I didn't understand what lay ahead with the Scary Bus Driver.

He didn't wait for anyone in the morning. If we weren't at the end of the driveway by a certain time, he would give two quick *honk-honks*. Then the doors of the bus would shut, the hand-controlled stop sign would go screeching back to a flattened position, he'd give a little annoyed face and with a roar of the tires the bus would disappear.

I can't be certain, but I'm fairly sure that even if he saw kids in the rearview mirror as he was pulling away he would step on the gas to leave them in the dust. I saw that happen many times to my fellow bus-riding friends, but seeing it is nothing compared to experiencing it firsthand.

My first such incident occurred early in my bus riding years, in the first or second grade. I remember being very engulfed in a certain episode of Sesame Street. So much so that 6:15 a.m. came and went, the *honk-honks* were drowned out by Bert, Ernie and the gang—and the rest is history. Needless to say, I missed the bus.

There were many mornings when my sister Lindsay and I just barely made it. We'd roll out of bed late, and then lose time frantically looking for a pair of matched socks and shoes! I'd grab my purple backpack, perhaps a piece of peanut butter toast, and run down our driveway, take a shortcut by jumping over the fence, and make it to the bus just in time to see the Scary Bus Driver's disapproving smirk. The doors would close, the stop sign go screeching back into place and we'd sigh— because we'd made it just in time.

And once you found your seat on the bus, there was no turning back! You didn't jump from seat to seat while the bus was moving. If you did, there were serious consequences. Unfortunately, it didn't take long for me to learn about those consequences.

One of my fellow bus riders and neighbors was a few years older than me. On a particularly gloomy day she dared me to switch seats while the bus was still in motion. My mind told me this was a bad idea, but peer pressure got the best of me and when I thought Scary Bus Driver wasn't looking I quickly moved to a different seat. It took only a moment for those eyes in the back of his head to see what I'd done and, to my misfortune, he gave me the scariest look. I began to tear up.

He yelled, too, and as soon as the bus came to a halt I was summoned to the front, to sit on the nasty bus steps for the remainder of the ride. Humiliated, I watched the rocks go by from an up-close and personal view. I promised myself it would never happen again.

It didn't.

Of all the moments during the hours of riding on that big yellow bus, one stands out the most. It wasn't a particular action, but a comment made by Scary Bus Driver that still baffles me to this day. I don't remember the actions leading up to this comment, but I assume we were all talking very loudly—on a day when we shouldn't have been talking at all.

Above the noise we heard Scary Bus Driver shout these very words: "Shut Up! I can't see!"

Now, in all my years I never thought sight and sound were in the same category. I didn't realize you had to be quiet to see the road. Apparently, Scary Bus Driver did. If we learned anything from that moment, it was to never question and to keep our mouths shut!

Although Scary Bus Driver was pretty scary year round, there was one fleeting moment each year that made him shine. That one moment made all his scary looks disappear. On the last day before Christmas break—when he would give all of us kids a big almond Hershey candy bar. It wasn't just a mini bar, but an extra-big Hershey bar. Year after year, it was the same treat—and I looked forward to it greatly! I'm certain very few bus drivers did such a thing, and my sister Lindsay swears he only gave the chocolate to his favorite bus riders.

Could it be I was one of his favorites? I received a big Hershey almond chocolate bar each year. Maybe I really was top notch in his book!

As a child, I thought Scary Bus Driver was the worst. I didn't understand why my father, who was on the school board, wouldn't do something about this guy! My parents kept telling me how great they felt knowing I was safe under his supervision. I didn't understand it at a young age, but now as a mother, it begins to make sense.

Scary bus driver, otherwise known as Jim, was simply trying to keep us safe. He didn't want me or the others to fly through the window in an accident, he needed us to be quiet so he could concentrate on the road, and he didn't want us to be late for school. He was doing the best job he could, and his methods worked. I'm happy to report that my fellow bus-riding friends and I were safe because of Jim.

All in all, I'll bet I rode at least 120,000 miles on that bus throughout a period of eight to twelve years. I didn't realize it as a kid, but Jim helped me make some of the best memories growing up. My sister, Lindsay, and I still get a great chuckle out of the phrase, "Shut up! I can't see!"

I guess Scary Bus Driver wasn't so bad after all.

Jim passed away a few years back. I wish I'd told him before he passed how much I appreciated his dedication to keeping each of us safe in that bus. If he were alive today, I'd give him a big hug—and a big Hershey almond chocolate bar to say "thanks!"

Leslie Means was born and raised on a farm in south central Nebraska. She now resides in Kearney, Nebraska, with her husband Kyle and daughters Ella and Grace. She is currently the co-host of a morning talk television show called *NTV's Good Life*. Leslie also enjoys writing children's books. Her first book, *Ella B. Bella and the Magic Pink Shoes*, was published and released during the spring of 2010.

Photo provided by Leslie Means

FRONT ROW K. Learmont, B. McFarland, J. Bahl, B.Rodenberg, M.Bragg, B. Snow
M. Bowden, S.Essick
SECOND ROW G. Vanden Bosch, J. Richards, D.Jacobsen, J.Groff, L.Christensen,
T.Smalley, S.Basler, K.Galema
THRID ROW Coach Whiting, A.McClain, J.Clark, L.Rush, S.Mumm, M.Woodrum,
M.Kroeger, B.Denker, L.Feauto
Photo provided by Judy Taber (J. Groff, Second Row)

SIX-ON-SIX

Judy Taber

Basketball was the winter social activity of small towns across Iowa in the 1950s and 1960s, with the girls' games often attracting larger crowds than the boys' games did. The larger urban schools didn't offer basketball as an organized sport until later.

We played six-on-six basketball—three forwards in one-half of the court and three guards in the other half. Only two dribbles were allowed, so one did not stand and dribble the ball while deciding what to do next. You either shot the ball at the basket, passed the ball to one of your teammates, or took your two dribbles to position yourself in another place on the court so that you could shoot or pass from there. Three-point shots had not yet been heard of.

By the early 1990s Iowa had switched to the full-court, five-on-five form of the game, and the big schools in the state had signed on and were offering organized girls' basketball as a school-sponsored sport.

My friends and I lived for basketball in the winter. We abided by our coach's rules and came to every practice. Missing practice was not an option. We were responsible for keeping our uniforms and our warm-up jackets clean, and we washed them after every Tuesday and Friday night game. Actually, our mothers did the washing, but we carried them home and back again, making sure that we had everything together.

It was 29 degrees outside on Monday, February 12, 1962. It had snowed three inches that day, on the heels of a weekend blizzard that had dumped eighteen inches of snow on the Lake Park community. No one had gone to Sunday school or church on Sunday, but that wasn't unusual in a northwest Iowa winter. However, by Monday evening, 584 people—302 adults and 282 students—had dug themselves out and traveled to the local high school to watch the Lake Park girls' basketball team take on Hartley in the first round of the sectional tournament. This was the first step toward being one of the Sweet Sixteen teams to advance to the state tournament in Des Moines. The state tourney would be played in "the barn," more properly known as Veteran's Memorial Auditorium.

The first round of our sectional tournament was held in the Lake Park gym. As a sophomore guard, I was excited to be playing a tournament game on our home court. We would have the home-court advantage, and we were playing Hartley, a good team that had beaten us twice during the regular season games. We were pumped for this third match-up and desperately wanted to win.

The game was close. At half-time, the score was tied.

It continued to be close, and toward the end of the last quarter a mix-up happened. One of the Hartley girls was called for traveling as she shot the ball. The ball went in the hoop, but the referee signaled "no basket," as the traveling call had occurred before the shot was taken.

Apparently the person running the scoreboard had looked down at the numbers to punch in two points and didn't see the referee make the no score call. Our coach didn't see it either, as he was giving instructions to one of our other players. Each team has a person who records all baskets made, free-throws made, fouls, etc. Neither of them had recorded the two-point basket.

I knew that the extra two points were on the scoreboard, but couldn't get the coach's attention. Part of the crowd watching knew also; the noise in the gym was deafening. The game continued and within a minute it was over. Final score on the scoreboard: Hartley – 68, Lake Park – 67. Only thing was, Hartley had those two extra points on the scoreboard that should not have been there.

By then our coach realized what had happened. The scorekeepers were checking and rechecking their records and both score books showed Lake Park – 67 and Hartley – 66.

What to do now?!

Nobody went home. The discussions continued. Finally, at about 11:00 p.m., a call was placed to Bernie Saggau, president of the Iowa High School Girls Athletic Union in Des

Moines. He contacted the board members and presented them with the information about the game.

The decision came at 1:30 a.m. The board of the Athletic Union gave the game to Hartley, "based on rule 10-7, section 7 of the rule book: Erroneously Counting or Canceling a Score—an equitable adjustment shall be attempted if the error is recognized prior to the second live ball after the error. Consumed time, points scored, and other activity which may occur prior to recognition of the error shall not be nullified."

So there it was. We had the most points, but we lost the game because of the mix-up in recording the score.

The Lake Park News reported the game on the front page of the February 15, 1962 edition, the article ending with, "Thus the scorekeepers' efforts in keeping a correct list of each individual's accomplishments on the basketball court is ruled null and void—and a waste of time—his records mean nothing according to the above rule!"

We felt cheated. This wasn't fair! Our coach apologized for not noticing the error sooner. My parents were sympathetic. Some of the fans were outraged. In the end, we all accepted the decision because it was based on a specific rule in the rule book. The decision had not been a subjective one.

Girls' basketball at Lake Park was done for the season. The uniforms were washed one last time and turned in. We turned our energies to small group music contest preparation.

Was there a life lesson in all of this? We learned that life is not always fair. We learned to move on and vow to do better next year.

And we cheered when Hartley got blasted out of the sectional tournament finals by Everly with a score of 105 to 66. How sweet it was!

Judy Taber, a retired adjunct university professor, and her husband, Gary, live in a home that they built on the south shore of Silver Lake at Lake Park, IA. Depending on the season and/or the weather, she can be found working in her extensive gardens or creating stained and fused glass art.

Photo courtesy of Kiron Kountry Library

BLIZZARD DAYS

Verla Klaessy

The sleigh bells on the harnesses of the huge work horses rang through the crisp air of the winter afternoon in 1936. As soon as I heard them I jumped up and down. It was my dad coming to get me from first grade at the country school house. I also knew he would give everyone living on our side of the school a ride home in the farm sled.

The bobsled was just a wagon box, wheels removed and sled runners attached, and pulled by our horses, Prince and Barney, who were my Dad's proud possessions. The horses worked summer and winter and were an important part of our farm. There were heavy blankets in the sled. A half dozen of us squealing and laughing kids snuggled together for the slick ride home over heavy snow. School had to be closed several times that winter as the winds blew and the snow whirled into heavy drifts. Snowplows were few on our country roads and often the shoveling of men and boys from neighboring farms was the only way to keep a path open on the road.

Little did we know, the worst was yet to come.

The next week it started snowing again. A fierce wind blew and howled around our chimney. We sat close to the oven of the big cook stove, added another sweater, popped corn and drank hot cocoa in the evenings. It wasn't unusual for a storm to last two or three days, with calmer winds in between. Dad still had to find his way to the barn to care for the cows and horses, feed the sheep and do the milking. He had attached a long rope to the porch and tied it to a large pole in the middle of the yard. Then another rope was fastened from the pole to the barn door. The rope would help him find his way from the barn to the house in the frenzy of the wind and snow. We were always happy when he returned to the house covered with snow, his cheeks red.

But during this storm, if the wind calmed at all it was only for a few hours. Then it would seem to gather strength, blowing violently and swirling the snow into huge drifts. Towering piles of snow covered the entire countryside. No one moved far from their homes. Loads of wood and cobs kept the cook stoves going constantly, usually with a delicious stew bubbling in a large kettle.

My mother, sister and I didn't venture out at all. We quickly tired of the constant whistling and squealing of the winds. To take our minds off the storm raging outside, Daddy told us stories and invented games. He told us about relatives we had not met who had been early settlers in Clay County.

He told us about one relative, an old man who'd possessed a furious temper and exploded without much provocation. It was well known not to disagree with him. The neighbor, upon seeing her first snowstorm of wild and hostile winds blowing the snow in all directions made the comment, "This terrible storm is just as awful and savage as old man Blizzard!"

Our family genealogy shows that we did have relatives named Blizzard, and according to family lore, one of them provided the basis of violent snow storms being called blizzards. We enjoyed the telling of the story and tried to picture that old man in one of his rages.

Week after week went by with zero-degree temperatures remaining even though the intense winds had subsided. There was no school, no mail and no travel anywhere. After six weeks, with groceries and fuel for the oil burner running low, my parents decided a trip to town was necessary.

My grandparents lived in Spencer, Iowa, eight miles from our farm. They had a huge house, which was well heated and even had electricity. We girls were becoming lethargic after weeks of no sunlight, being constantly housebound and bored beyond anything we had known before.

The day finally arrived when the winds were silent, the temperature had risen above 25 degrees and we were going in the bobsled to town. What excitement as we were dressed in several layers of clothing! Mother heated bricks in the oven to keep our feet warm for the trip and heavy blankets, including a couple made from horse hair, were piled by the door, ready for us to pick them up and take them along for warmth.

The plan was to drive across the fields, as none of the roads were yet passable.

My Dad talked to his brother by telephone and made plans to drive across the fields. My uncle would drive his car to meet us on the highway, which had been opened. My sister and I would go to our grandparents' house while our parents shopped for groceries and supplies.

Prince and Barney were harnessed to the bobsled, wearing their jingle bells. The horses pulled us across the snowy field over a heavy crust of snow frozen hard from the many days of freezing temperatures. We were amazed as, along the way, we saw only the tops of houses and barns. Telephone poles stuck out only a few feet as we zoomed by in our sled. The horses never broke through the top crust of the snow.

Finally we arrived at the highway. There was the car, waiting for us. My uncle whisked us away to the grandparents' home. Along the way we saw that piles and piles of snow had been scooped by hand from the city streets. Other teams of horses stood on Main Street, waiting for their owners to make the return trip home over the snowy land.

Grandma had hot homemade cookies waiting for us. Quickly we shed our layers of clothing and delighted in the warmth and bright lights of her house. When the adults returned later they told of the train being immersed in huge drifts. Dozens of men had used scoops and shovels to remove the snow around the wheels and the tracks so it could get moving again. It had been carrying fuel, mail and other essentials.

Too soon it was time to head back so we would reach home before dark. Grandma reheated the bricks, and reluctantly we dressed again in our heavy clothing, climbed in the car for the short ride to where we'd tethered the horses. Prince and Barney were patiently waiting beside a short length of telephone pole sticking out from the snow bank.

A light snow was falling as we started once again across the field. The rhythm of the bells and the jogging of the horses lulled us into a tranquil mood. The reheated bricks and warm blankets, along with the excitement of the trip, made us sleepy, and soon my little sister and I were napping.

It was six weeks before school opened once more. Many hours of hand scooping had opened lanes and roads for traffic once again. Traveling through tunnels of snow was common on many roads.

We never forgot this adventure, or the courage of men and women who withstood such a horrendous time while caring for their families and livestock.

Those same sleigh bells that Prince and Barney wore are jingling by my back door now, attached to a heavy leather belt.

I often think of those days and my distant relatives—the Blizzards.

Verla Klaessy grew up on a farm near Spencer, Iowa, in the 1930s, graduated from Spencer High School and attended William Penn University in Oskaloosa, Iowa. She has been married to Earl for 62 years and enjoys writing as a retirement hobby.

THE BLIZZARD OF 1975—
A NEAR CAT . . . ASTROPHE

Roger Stoner

"The National Weather Service is predicting a major winter storm—" were the words we heard coming from my car radio as my friend, Rick, and I drove to work that Friday morning, January 10th, 1975, *"—but frankly, I just can't see it!"* Eldon Kanago, the weatherman on Spencer, Iowa's KICD radio station, finished his weather forecast for the day, calling for a chance of flurries with moderate wind speeds of 15 to 20 miles per hour.

I shut the radio off as I parked my car in the Eaton Corporation parking lot, and we went into the factory to go to work, just like any other day.

There are few windows in the factory, but people had their radios on and we didn't need to look out to see that Eldon the Weatherman had missed his forecast of earlier that morning. By noon he was describing the major winter storm he had doubted: *"—several inches of snow have fallen. Winds blowing 50 miles per hour with gusts even higher make it impossible to even measure the amount of snowfall thus far this morning."*

It was time to leave. We evacuated the factory like rats leaving a sinking ship, everyone scurrying to their vehicles. It was an orderly line as we patiently left the lot and turned onto the road. All of the vehicles ahead of me turned east toward Spencer, either going to their homes or to a safe and warm motel room.

But not me. I turned west, heading for home in Peterson, a 25-mile journey. Several people told me I was crazy and warned me that I'd never make it.

"Visibility is only a few feet!"

"There are no snow plows running!"

"Only an idiot would try driving to Peterson in a storm like this!"

They were probably right. But you see, I'd gotten married a mere three weeks earlier, on December 20, 1974, and my 18-year-old bride was all alone in our house, waiting for my return.

I drove a 1972 blue Toyota Corona. It had a 4-cylinder engine with 98 horsepower, and the guy who sold it to me said it featured *rack & pinion* steering (whatever that is). Since it was two-wheel drive, I had 300 pounds of bagged sand and a snow shovel in the trunk and come hell, high water, or 15-foot-high snow drifts for that matter, I wasn't going to disappoint her by not making it home.

Rick and I left the factory at 12:00 noon and started a long, slow trip. It was a total "white-out." Visibility was one or maybe two car lengths at best. The road was completely snow-covered. The ditches were full, level with the road, and I had to feel my way along, searching for the hard surface beneath the snow.

Several times I felt my tires drop off the road onto one shoulder or the other, and I quickly steered back onto the road and away from the ditch.

Shortly after we had turned onto the snow-covered road going south at the Everly corner, Rick announced that he had to, "pee like a racehorse." I stopped without bothering to pull over. There was no one else crazy enough to be out on the roads that day. When Rick opened his door to get out, the wind blasted it out of his hands and wrapped it around until it too was pointing south, the door handle rubbing up against the front fender. It took both of us to push it back. Luckily the hinge wasn't broken and I was able to latch it for the remainder of the trip home.

We were about 14 miles north of Peterson when I noticed that I could see the tops of the high-line poles on both sides of the road. Using the pole tops as guides, I was able to keep the car in the middle of the road by keeping an equal distance between them, and I had no more near-misses with the shoulders.

It was 4:00 p.m. when we crested the top of the hill and rolled down into the valley where Peterson lies, protected a bit from the wind. But it had started to snow again and the wind, still blowing 50 miles per hour, was depositing a lot of the snow from the flat land to the north into the valley.

Rick jumped into his truck and took off for home, which was a couple of miles south of town, and I began scooping a path to my garage so I could get my faithful old Toyota out of the weather. An hour later I entered our house into the welcoming arms of my new young wife.

Some would later refer to the blizzard of 1975 as a storm of catastrophic consequences. People were stranded far from their homes. Some froze to death. Some were killed by the several rare, wintertime tornadoes that sprang up from the weather conditions that had caused the storm. It snowed and the wind blew hard that night, continuing all day Saturday and through Saturday night. It didn't let up much until near noon on Sunday, January 12th.

For me, it wasn't all that unpleasant, being snowed in, just the wife and I. Our relationship was new enough that we still had plenty of things to talk about. We planned for the future and shared our dreams and goals. We never lost power, so we could have read books and magazines or watched television on our black and white TV. We did lose one of our three television channels when the tall communications tower in Sioux Falls, South Dakota went down in the wind, but as I mentioned, we had only been married for three weeks so I didn't watch that much TV and hardly noticed the loss of channel 11.

The phone rang Sunday around noon. I answered it.

"Roger," the voice on the other end stated, "I need help."

I immediately recognized the voice of our next-door neighbor, Bill.

Bill was a widower in his eighties, with no relatives in the area. Upon hearing his plea for help, I felt a sudden pang of guilt for not thinking to check in on him during the storm. I slammed down the phone and began bundling up in my warm clothes.

"Bill needs help!" I shouted to my wife, which brought a look of concern to her face as she came out of the bedroom.

I finished dressing and rushed out of the house to the back porch, where I grabbed up my shovel and tried to open the door. Three feet of snow was blocking it, so I removed the storm window in the door and stepped through it. The snow was hip-deep and I struggled to wade through it until I finally made it to Bill's back door.

I scooped like a madman, imagining all kinds of horrible things that may have befallen my elderly neighbor, while I had been whiling away the storm in newlywed bliss. A broken hip, a broken arm, a broken leg, a heart attack or maybe a stroke. Or maybe he had cut himself and was bleeding to death!

I had to get that door scooped free and get into that house!

Finally I shoveled the last few scoops of snow out from in front of his door. I threw down the shovel and jerked the door open.

Bill was standing there waiting for me. He had a big orange tomcat cradled in one arm and he was holding a long rubber hose with a little bulb on the end of it in his other hand.

"I need you to hold this cat while I give him an enema," he stated calmly, adding, "He hasn't crapped in his litter box since this goddamn storm hit."

It took me a minute to regain my composure.

"Bill," I said. "I'm not going to hold that cat while you shove that hose where the sun don't shine!"

"Why not?" he asked.

"He has claws and teeth!" I answered. And I swear that cat looked me straight in the eyes, flexed his claws, bared his fangs and growled at me. "He'll rip me to pieces!"

"Well, then I'll hold him and you shove the hose in," Bill offered.

"Look Bill, the snow is hip-high all the way from here to Spencer and there is no way an ambulance is going to haul either one of us to the hospital when that cat gets done with us, so I'm not going to try to help you give it an enema," I stated firmly. Then, remembering my guilty feelings from fifteen minutes ago, I added, "Is there anything else I can do for you?"

He thought for a minute and asked, "Could you walk down to Hansen's Market and get me a bottle of Milk of Magnesia laxative? Maybe I can feed him some of that."

"That I can do," I said.

And I did, thus avoiding what could have changed an idyllic weekend with my new wife into the catastrophic event that the Blizzard of 1975 was for so many other people.

Roger Stoner published *The Peterson Patriot* for over 15 years and wrote a weekly column called "Roger's Remarks." His short stories have been published in three anthologies and he has had two articles published in magazines. His first book, *Life with My Wife: The Memoir of an Imperfect Man* has recently been released, and his current work, *Horse Woman's Child,* a full-length historical novel, is in progress. Roger and his wife, Jane, live in Peterson, Iowa.

Photo provided by Roger Stoner

Photo provided by Pat Larsen

JOURNEY THROUGH THE VALLEY OF DEATH

Pat Larsen

On Friday, January 10, 1975, the most violent blizzard of the century blasted through northwest Iowa and the surrounding area, leaving behind thousands of dead cattle, 56 storm-related deaths and 12 inches of snow. It was called, by the Minneapolis Weather Bureau, the worst storm since the 1800s for the areas of Iowa, Minnesota, Nebraska and South Dakota.

What started as an ordinary Iowa winter day turned into a 20-hour journey that almost cost me my life.

It was snowing moderately that morning as my husband, Eldon, left for work and three of our four kids left for school. By 11:00 a.m. the schools were dismissing and children were being returned home.

The storm grew in violence hour by hour as the winds gusted to more than 50 m.p.h.

At around 9:00 p.m. my husband called to say he planned to spend the night at his workplace, Spencer Foods, because the streets were blocked. When I told him I'd come by snowmobile to get him, his comment was, "You stay in where it's safe and warm. I'll be home as soon as the storm lets up."

I assured him I'd be just fine with the snowmobile. "Don't worry," I insisted, "I'm not afraid."

Looking back, maybe a little fear at that moment would have served me well.

I bundled up in my snowmobile gear and set out to get him. After dodging many stalled vehicles and towering snow-drifts, my nightmare began. As I approached an intersection of 16th Street and West 4th Avenue in total darkness, I encountered a stalled pickup truck. The huge snowdrifts and extremely poor visibility forced me to alter my course.

As I began to U-turn around the pickup, the driving snow caused me to lose all sense of direction. I felt as though I were tumbling around in a whirling funnel of a tornado made of snow. In my confusion, instead of a U-turn I made a complete circle, running smack into a large snowdrift.

I was stuck.

Fear set in when I couldn't free my snowmobile from the deep snow, but I heard a voice in my head saying, "Don't panic, stay calm and you'll be just fine!"

I surveyed my situation and decided on a plan of action. I could see the chain link fence that surrounded the racetrack near the east end of the Clay County fairgrounds, but little else. I knew the landmarks and began to gain a sense of direction. I reasoned that by following that racetrack fence three-fourths of a block south I would find the intersection, and just beyond that would be houses and safety.

But after walking only about ten feet through waist-deep snow, the blizzard still raging around me, I quickly came to the stark realization that I would not get far in these conditions. It would be best to return to the snowmobile, I decided, so that, in the event that I froze to death, searchers would be able to find my body before the spring thaw.

A morbid thought, maybe, but certainly a possibility.

I sat down beside my snowmobile and dug a trench in the snow, hoping the machine would provide some sort of a windbreak from the storm. The wind thundered over the fence above me, the sound like roaring water crashing over Niagara Falls.

I found comfort in reciting the Lord's Prayer and the 23rd Psalm, both taught to me by my grandmother when I was a young child. I settled into a false sense of security, confident that my husband would come for me at daybreak

During that long, cold night, many thoughts raced wildly through my mind, though survival remained my top priority. Several times I became hysterical, bargaining with God. After many hours of despair I finally accepted my situation and waited for the storm to die down.

Knowing that I mustn't sleep, I thought of our four children, family camping trips we'd taken, and special moments with my husband. I remembered to wiggle my fingers and toes periodically to keep the circulation going, as these are the first to freeze and I didn't intend for them to become popsicles.

At one point I found myself pounding on each ankle with the opposite foot to try to get some feeling back into my toes.

At daybreak the storm was still raging as violently as ever. I became very depressed then, as I'd been clinging to the belief that morning would bring an end to the storm, and to my nightmare. I kept praying, "Please God, save me. I'm not ready to die. I still have things I want to do!"

Typical behavior of someone staring death in the eye.

During the day I heard snowmobiles not far away and knew people were looking for me. Once I heard voices very near. They belonged to my brother, brother-in-law and a family friend, who, I learned later, were tethered together by a rope, searching for me. I called out to them, to no avail.

Several times during that long, bitter cold, dismal day, I struggled out of my snow trench to check the visibility, but it was always the same—absolutely ZERO. Dejected, I went back to my trench to wait out the fury of the storm.

By late afternoon I was so cold and shivering so violently that I developed muscle cramps in my thighs. Knowing that the temperature was expected to drop to 20 below zero that night, I knew I wouldn't last another night outside.

I began to pray, "Dear God, if I'm going to survive, you'll have to show me the way. I can't do this alone."

At that moment I felt suddenly calm. Something prompted me to stand-up, pry off my iced-over goggles with numb hands encased in frozen mittens.

I looked to my left. I saw a strange, eerie glow, a wispy vision that took on the illusion of my deceased grandmother.

I cried out, "Please take me with you! I'm so cold and weak. I can't go on."

No words were spoken, but a feeling of peace and tranquility descended upon me and I felt the presence gently urging me to seek shelter, as it wasn't my time to be with her.

This was truly the divine intervention from God that I'd prayed for. Then the sky grew very bright and the wind quit blowing. I saw the stalled pickup truck. In that moment I knew where the houses were and that safety lay just beyond.

The first steps I took were agonizing. I was disoriented and dizzy, one of the early signs of hypothermia.

I fell several times but managed to get up. I walked slowly on top of the crusted snow, making my way to the street, determined to save myself.

I crawled and stumbled to a house, falling again and again. I reached the garage and frantically pounded on the door. At first no one heard me, then a woman appeared.

The door was frozen shut and she called out to me to go to the front door. I was so weak that I didn't think I'd make it those last 25 feet, but with safety so near I wasn't about to quit.

She opened the door and I fell, covered with a thick layer of ice and snow, to the floor, frightening her two young children with my grotesque appearance. I told her my name and she immediately called the police department. Then she came back to me and gently removed my helmet, facemask and mittens. She wrapped my hands in a soft, dry towel and covered me with a cozy blanket.

Soon after her call, a police officer arrived, followed by my husband. An ambulance arrived about an hour later, following a path made by two payloaders and a snowplow that had dug and clawed their way through the still-raging storm.

When I arrived at the hospital there were nurses, doctors and the warmest bed I'd ever felt waiting for me. My body temperature was so low it didn't register on the thermometer; oxygen kept my lungs from collapsing, and I was kept awake to prevent my going into shock.

A sense of euphoria came over me, as I was enveloped in blankets much like a caterpillar encased in a cocoon.

I'd suffered extreme frostbite on both feet and hands, my right thumb was frozen to the bone and I had third degree ice burns on both wrists. I wear these scars yet today, as a constant reminder of my brush with death.

I was more fortunate than a friend who lost his life in the same storm. My only losses were of my fingernails, toenails and a lot of skin. In time I recovered physically, but it took a very long time to recover emotionally. Sometimes I still suffer relapses of fear and panic, especially during blizzards.

During those long, cold 20 hours, I tried to remain calm, though at times I was certain I was going to die. The comforting words of the 23rd Psalm provided me with the strength and courage I needed to survive. Many prayers were said for me during my ordeal and it was by God's grace that I was given the will to survive and received the chance to continue my life.

I became a celebrity of sorts, my story appearing on the national news and published in a lot of newspapers.

It's been 35 years since my ordeal. Blizzards and howling winds still make me nervous and edgy, but I give thanks for each new day and believe my life was changed dramatically by my journey.

Pat Larsen has always loved to write but never thought about doing anything with it. When she retired in 2000, she was looking for a way to fill her time, so she enrolled in some creative writing classes at ILCC and became interested in doing short stories. Through her writing she has met new friends and looks forward to meeting more.

Photo provided by Irene Jaeger

HE KNEW

Irene Jaeger

Today is dark and dreary, with rain keeping us out of the fields. This day reminds me of similar days, long ago, when my brother, Don, and I would lie up in the loft of the hay barn and watch it rain. In the spring we would whittle wooden pegs from pieces of hickory wood Dad would split just for that purpose.

Before the days of herbicides, farmers cultivated between the corn rows for weed control. The pegs were used to hold cultivator shovels in place, and we'd fill a big toolbox with them. When cultivators inevitably hit rocks, the pegs would give way, to avoid breaking the shovels, and we could immediately replace them. Some days we hit so many rocks, we came home with a near-empty toolbox.

My dad was sick, so I worked in the fields with my brothers, while my older sister worked in the house with Ma. We'd get up early in the morning to milk the cows, then after breakfast my brothers and I would feed our horses, get them harnessed and hooked up to the cultivator, then work the corn fields until noon. We'd lead the teams back to the watering tank to drink, then go have dinner. Ma always had a delicious home-cooked meal waiting for us, and we really enjoyed her cooking.

When dinner was over, Don and I would take our teams back to the fields until it was time to bring the cows in from the pasture for their evening milking. We'd head to the barn, take off the harnesses and groom the horses, get them fed and watered, milk the cows again, and then head to the house for supper. Often we would sit outside as a family to talk about our day. I miss those times of visiting. Today, we're usually too busy to take the time to sit and visit with our family and friends.

Don and I were waiting for our new corn picker to arrive. Dad had ordered it during WWII, so it took us a long time to get it. I remembered the previous harvest, when Don and I had picked the corn by hand. That was 1944. Using a steel peg, we'd grab an ear of corn, shuck it, and throw it in the wagon box. It was a lot of work, but we enjoyed working together, and knew that we'd have a corn picker for next year's harvest. We were excited!

Finally, the corn picker arrived. Don, who was a very good mechanic, came to the house and asked his "grease monkey" sister to come help him get the new picker greased and running for next season. I loved helping him, and before long we got that new picker ready to go.

Don told me, "If I don't see it working now, I'll never get to see it."

I thought that was a strange thing for him to say, but we took the picker out and gave it a trial run. Of course, that year's corn was already picked, but at least he could see how the new machine worked.

Every fall, Don and I would remove the shovels from the cultivator and store them until the next year. We always stored the shovels over the slops' shed door. This particular time, Don put the shovels up and then said to me," Irene, remember where I put these for next year, because I won't be here."

Again I thought that was strange, since we usually kept them there anyway, but I just nodded, and we went on into the house for supper.

A short while later, my brother took sick. Pa and Ma took him to the doctor, who put Don in the hospital. The doctors there said it was his appendix, that it had burst and he had peritonitis.

Don never came home. He passed away early that April, before he ever got to pick corn with the new picker. Somehow, my nineteen-year-old brother had known he wouldn't be around for harvest that year.

I was really glad that we'd greased the corn picker together, and that he'd seen it run.

Irene Jaeger is the youngest of six children, raised on a farm in Guttenberg, Iowa. Growing up during the depression, she and her siblings didn't have much, but they always had love from their wonderful parents. In September 2010 she turned eighty years old, and still lives on the farm.

Photo provided by Irene Jaeger

Photo provided by Marilyn Ford

THE HIRED MAN

Marilyn Ford

My parents were farmers in North Dakota during the Great Depression. They were "dirt poor." Gas lanterns for light, a coal stove for heat, and running water meant you ran faster to the well. Food came from the garden and was preserved. Cando was the big town for shopping. The word "poor" wasn't spoken, only the future plans for "next year when . . ."

It was winter, 1940, and Christmas was fast approaching. The 14-year-old "hired man," Robert, liked working with my father but he missed his parents and his brothers and sisters. His family lived many miles away and he seldom saw them. To be a hired man meant a lot to Robert and at the end of every month he sent his paycheck to his parents.

I was five years old and I followed him everywhere. It was true I had a brother, but he was very sickly and unable to play, and so it was that Robert allowed me to follow him around, asking my endless questions about the animals and "Why are you doing that?"

He liked to work in the barn, and of course there was always work to do, from cleaning the stalls to feeding and milking the cows. He also put down fresh bedding for the horses each night. He would climb up into the haymow, where he'd push hay into the stalls below. The barn cats would leap into the hay searching for little mice.

It was in the barn where Robert told me he would have a barn of his own one day. I said I wanted a barn and a tractor because then Dad wouldn't have to walk behind the plow.

As the windy, cold days of December enfolded the farm, I was no longer allowed to be outside alone. I stayed inside with my mother and brother while Robert and my father worked together. When the day ended they came in to warm their bodies by the cook stove.

When he was in the house, Robert didn't talk much and he never talked about having a barn of his own some day.

My brother was very sick with rheumatic fever. Sometimes I heard my parents talking about my brother getting a damaged heart if he didn't stay in bed. They were very worried, and the house was kept quiet during the day. I cut out pictures of animals from the farm magazines, then pasted them onto paper using paste made of flour and water. My wish was to be in the barn, hearing the sounds, smelling the hay and playing with the nameless barn cats. But my biggest wish was for my brother to get well, so my parents would smile and laugh again. Somehow I knew that Christmas would be plain.

Robert didn't talk about Christmas or about his parents, but one day I heard him ask my dad if he had some nails and a saw he might use. Dad told him to look around the shop and help himself to nails, and to use the saw and hammer that were hanging on the wall.

Robert went out into the unheated shop and found the tools he needed, plus an empty apple box. He also noticed a can of paint that was a strange shade of green. He asked Dad if he would be allowed to use the paint. Dad said, "Go ahead, but I don't think it is any good because it has been in the cold too long."

During the next few days I saw very little of Robert. He seemed to be very busy with the animals and working in the shop. I wondered what he was doing in there, and speculated that he was making a gift for his parents.

I heard him ask Dad for some private conversation time. Robert talked to Dad about Christmas and asked if he would be able to return to his parent's home for the holidays. It had been several months since he had seen them and with Christmas and all, he would like to be with them. But if that wasn't possible, he said he understood. Dad said by all means he could go home. Then I heard Robert whisper something about, "Don't forget about something in the shop," and if Dad would make sure . . .

Dad smiled.

94

The next morning he hitched the horses to the "stoneboat/hack."

During summer months, horses pulled the stoneboat sled through the fields for "rock pick'un." Family members helped pick up rocks to clear the fields for cultivation. We deposited them onto the sled, and the horses towed them out of the way to be piled in another spot.

When the roads became snow-covered, Dad mounted a hack onto the stoneboat for winter transportation. It was a constructed box with a small door, a front window, and openings for reins to pass through from the horses to the driver on the inside. Passengers sat inside on plank seats and covered themselves with cowhide robes for protection from the cold weather. That was our transportation to school, visiting neighbors or attending church.

Shortly before Christmas, Dad and Robert entered our hack, covered their bodies with cowhide robes, and drove off into the cold. Robert was going to have Christmas with his parents and his brothers and sisters.

Two days later it was Christmas morning. A surprise was waiting for me. There was a miniature green barn, complete with a hayloft peeking out from under the Christmas tree. The doors at the end of the barn even opened and closed. I quickly gathered my pasted animals from the farm magazines and placed them next to the green barn.

"Look, everybody the hired man made this for me!"

Robert, the hired man, age fourteen, had given away his dream to me.

It wasn't a plain Christmas at all. It was the best.

My father lived to the age of 102. He told me that although only fourteen years of age and five foot two, Robert was one of his very best hired men. As Dad said, "He worked like a grown man."

Marilyn Ford is a writer of short stories, and writer and presenter of monologues. Youth and aging issues form the bones of her stories renewing memories for people of all ages. She and her husband, Ernie, live on the Olympic Canal in Washington State. They are the parents of three adult sons and have two grandsons and two step-grandsons.

Photo courtesy of Butternut Ridge Miniature Donkeys

Legend tells us the donkey that carried Jesus into Jerusalem on Palm Sunday followed Him to Calvary. Appalled by the sight of Jesus on the cross, the donkey turned away but could not leave. It is said that the shadow of the cross fell upon the shoulders and back of the donkey. A cross marking found on many donkeys today remains a testimony of the love and devotion of a humble, little donkey.

Courtesy Butternut Ridge Miniature Donkeys
Peru, NY

MY FRIEND ELMER

Isaiah Gray

Haw Hee-Haw Hee Haw Hee!
That melodious sound once came "burro-ing" from the barn. The sound was a reminder of feeding time, and also a warm welcome every time I arrived home. I never thought of how magnificent and manipulative a donkey could be, nor have I ever been a person to reconcile coincidences. Things happen, and they are bound to happen for a reason. But after the purchase of Elmer, my family would never be the same.

It was early April of 2002, as we sat on the cold wood bleachers inside the show arena. We were at one of many exotic animal sales we enjoyed on weekends. My father watched the proceedings intently as I shivered with my back turned toward the western breeze. The large animals were up to sell when a larger-scale, miniature donkey walked into the ring. To me he appeared to be nothing more than just your regular donkey. But there was something so appealing about him my dad began to bid. Perhaps it was the mark of the cross on his back and shoulders.

The bidding war was a simple one, rarely seen at these sales. It was between Dad and another gentleman a couple of rows down. It ended with the auctioneer asking for the winner's number, but to his surprise both men raised their cards!

The bidding continued with the other man, who agreed to raise his bid. Then it was up to Dad. I could see in his eyes that he was considering all aspects of the situation, but it wasn't until this donkey turned his head and looked my father in the eyes that he knew what the answer had to be. With a simple nod, the battle of the bidders ended with my dad being victorious. The elderly woman who'd owned this donkey presented to us a paper with its name and year of birth.

And Elmer was officially adopted into our family.

Small farming, or niche farming as I have often heard it called, is something of what we do. On our farm you'll see a variety of animals, ranging from ducks to goats, guineas to llamas.

The barnyard was in for a surprise the night when a six hundred-pound, attitude-wielding fuzzy animal came rolling out of the trailer. As many people know, bringing a new animal into the herd often leads to an immediate pecking-order ritual. We had ourselves a large male llama who was the self-proclaimed alpha-male of the barnyard, but he was about to be dethroned.

Elmer nonchalantly strolled into the pen, just minding his own business. That's when Wilbur, our llama, made his first mistake. As it would seem, sneaking up on a donkey is not always the brightest or safest way to get his attention. A simple bite on the ear from Wilbur sent Elmer spiraling, and with a bray, a jump, and the sound of a double-barrel shotgun connecting with Wilbur's jaw, a new dynasty had begun.

Wilbur would live to see another day, but he would spend the rest of his life with a one-tooth smile and painless bite.

Elmer reigned over all the animals, for they all feared the dreaded kick. But, though he appeared to be a hard-nosed jackass, in truth he had a mellow disposition, and he cared dearly for the man who'd brought him to this little side of heaven known as Iowa.

I am yet to see this from either of our other two donkeys, which could only mean it's not the usual characteristic. Elmer had an aura of arrogance and expected his ego to be filled. If Dad did not greet his pet first, then for the rest of the day Dad would get the "cold butt."

The cold butt is much like the cold shoulder, but rather than turning his head Elmer would turn completely around and only let Dad look at his other end. No matter what direction he walked, Elmer's overfed behind mocked Dad's very presence.

Regardless of the years we put up with this behavior, Elmer still did no wrong in my father's eyes. Dad was so infatuated with this donkey that he carried himself with an overwhelming pride. Every trip to town became a twenty-mile "Elmero the Burro" serenade. If we happened to bump into somebody, all we'd hear was Elmer this and Elmer that. I could hardly believe that this donkey had corrupted my very own father. Perhaps Dad really believed the Legend of the Donkey Cross, and assumed that the hand of God had touched Elmer.

Eventually this inseparable duo would meet an untimely parting of the ways. On a cold, wet March morning as I returned home from work, I went out to the barn to begin chores. As I opened the door and walked in with a pitchfork full of hay I saw the most painful, gut-wrenching sight—Elmer was down, and he wasn't getting up. There'd been no bray when I got home and no bray when I'd gone into the barn. I could only fear the worst as I looked down upon his motionless body.

I had to do something. I jumped inside the pen and rushed over to his side. Elmer's breaths, although labored, were still coming.

How had this well-loved, middle-aged donkey friend suddenly become sick? I tried pushing him up onto his feet, to no avail. So I then stood off to his side and wrapped my arms around his chest and, with a deep breath and a prayer, picked Elmer up. I set him gently on his feet and held him until he regained his balance.

He was very weak. I brought him his feed and water while I anxiously awaited my father's return. I gave Elmer a vow not to leave his side. If this were to be his last day, he would see his master one last time.

The winter had been harsh and took a toll on the animals. We called our vet to come have a look, and Elmer was diagnosed with pneumonia. We spent the next two days primarily out in the barn with our beloved friend. My father and I force-fed and watered him for two days. We had him vaccinated and laid blankets on him, yet his chance of survival seemed slim.

Then, on a cold Sunday afternoon, we went out to feed him again, hoping this time he could eat on his own. Little did we know Elmer's bite wouldn't necessarily be for his food. The funnel we meticulously placed in his mouth was pushed aside by his tongue, and Dad's fingers took its place.

At first Dad was calm and just said Elmer was biting, but then his voice changed to a blood-curdling scream. It was a scream like that of a horror movie victim. The hair on the back of my neck stood straight up. Never had I dreamt a human could make such a frightening sound.

My mother, who was nearby, handed me a hammer. I tried forcing it into the half-inch gap between Elmer's jaws. No luck. After the failed attempt with the hammer my mom shouted, "Crowbar!"

For whatever reason, Dad had brought a three-foot long crowbar into the barn the night before, and it was still there. I grabbed hold of the crowbar and stuck it through the ever-decreasing gap between Elmer's teeth. I pulled and pried for what seemed like hours, with little luck. All I kept saying, over and over, was, "Lord, give me strength."

Then for whatever reason, Elmer's jaws budged just enough for Dad to remove his fingers. Some may say I finally got the proper leverage, but I feel that God gave me the strength I needed.

After this ordeal, instead of being concerned about his fingers, the first thing Dad asked was, "You didn't break his jaw did you?"

I was dumbfounded! How could he be worried about his magnificent friend when his fingers had been so thoroughly and painfully smashed?

And so it was that a donkey, which was supposedly touched by the hand of God, bit the hand that fed him. Dad went to the emergency room with two well-crushed fingers. The doctor told him that I had probably saved his fingers.

As for Elmer, he died that night. The farm just doesn't quite seem the same without him. No longer are we welcomed home by that bray, reminding us that a fat donkey waited.

Elmer has been deeply missed, and though we may buy another donkey some day, he'll never be replaced.

Isaiah Gray still lives on an acreage near Everly, Iowa. During high school he was active in 4-H, FFA, and football. His family raises miniature donkeys, but no longer get their hands close to a donkey's mouth.

BOTTLE LAMB TO BUNTING BUCK

Delores Swanson

I believe that anyone who knows anything about farming will agree—it's a gamble against Mother Nature and a potentially dangerous occupation involving large machines and sometimes dangerous animals. It's also a treasure of wonderful memories, some good, some bad and many very humorous. As I have grown into my elder years and we have our family get-togethers, it's the humorous memories that are recalled over and over again.

I was born on a farm in northwest Iowa near the little town of May City, 85 years ago. I was the oldest of three girls, with no brothers. My next youngest sister, Lorraine, was six years my junior, so with my being the oldest I was expected to watch out for my little sister. Naturally, when something untimely happened it was my fault, because I was "old enough to know better."

When I got old enough to go outside and help my father, I was more than willing because that meant I was not always responsible for Lorraine. And I loved the outdoors, so whenever Dad needed help, I was happy to be his right-hand man.

During that time, my father had a flock of about one hundred to one hundred fifty ewes that he'd bought out west. I helped with the care of the young lambs, docking (cutting off their tails) and assisting with the castrations, though I was told to never to tell anyone about it because young girls were not supposed to know about *that*.

I also assisted with lambing, when necessary, which also was a no-no. I firmly believe that any child, born and raised on a working farm, learns more about nature and many other things than any town kid ever really knows. As a result of my closeness with the sheep, any time there was an orphan lamb it was my job to take care of it. It seems to be the nature of sheep to not claim the first of a set of twins, especially if they are born in the open or if the mother, in her labor, gets separated from the first born. With a flock of that many sheep, many times I had my own flock of little bottle-lambs following me wherever I went because I was their "mama."

One year my father wanted a black-faced ram, which would be an upgrade from the white-faced rams we'd always had. When he had the chance to purchase a black-faced male bottle lamb, it became just another in my entourage.

All went well as this black-faced lamb grew into a fine specimen of a male sheep. He was big boned, had perfect body contours, a nice fleece and looked to be just what the doctor ordered.

That was great, except for one fact. My mother's younger brother, Clarence, who was living with us at the time, and my father's younger brother, Richard, who farmed the "home" place and worked with my father, thought it was great fun to teach that innocent young ram to bunt. The farther back he would back up and then bunt into their outspread hands, the funnier it was to them.

Such fun they had, until the young ram became part of the team of "masters" of the flock. Buck, as we'd named him, wanted to be "king of the hill." We split the flock into different yards during breeding season. But still Buck thought he was boss, so my father always had to keep one eye on him when working in the flock that Buck owned. I was not allowed to be in the yard with him. Instead, I acted as the lookout. Whenever Buck showed signs of impending bunt—he would stand, looking at his next victim and shaking his head—I was to yell so Dad could defend himself with a pail or basket or whatever he had in his hands.

Everything went well until the breeding season was over and the rams had to be separated from the ewes. The white-faced rams were delegated to an area in the grove and Buck was put on the house lawn. He made a great lawnmower, which was a boon to me, but we had to be sure the yard gates were secured when we went through them. He'd quickly learned that if he bunted hard enough he could snap the spring on the gate, so we had to fasten the gates with a length of chain and a hook.

One sunny summer Sunday morning, when we came home from church, we immediately noticed that Buck was not at the gate to greet us. The screen door to the back porch had a hole in it.

Yes, you guessed it. Buck was not only *not* in the porch, but had actually gotten into the house.

My mother was the first one in the house, calling for Buck. She heard him answer from the top of the stairs. There he stood, looking down, but evidently afraid to tackle the first descending step. My father went up the stairs and got behind him. With a not-so-gentle push, he got Buck started down the steps. The first couple of steps went as intended but then Buck evidently lost his footing, tumbling down the last two thirds of the way, into the kitchen and out the door.

We soon discovered, much to our chagrin, that the black-faced ram had been in every room in the house expect one bedroom, and had only missed that one because the door had been closed. While Mom prepared dinner, Dad and I cleaned up every room with a broom and dustpan while Lorraine sought out the "accidents."

I'm not so sure that our having been to church that morning was of much value to my parents, especially Mom. She was a very good housekeeper and this just meant extra work for her, and on a Sunday besides.

About the time Lorraine had reached the age of six or seven, she was long-legged and a very fast runner, thank goodness. She needed the speed when it came to Buck. For some reason he seemed to have it in for her. If she wasn't watching him, he would knock her down. I remember one time in particular when she was tagging along behind me, as usual. I heard her scream and looked around to see Buck chasing her. The car was parked in front of the gate, which had to be secured because of him, remember?

I opened the car door and got in. Lorraine ran past the door and around the front of the car. I opened the other door but she couldn't make the corner to get in. Around and around they went, until Mom came out of the house with a broom to check what all the screaming was about. She had to unfasten the gate before she could get close enough to hit Buck over the head. That stopped him, but again, I got blamed because I was old enough to know better. I still don't know what for, but such is the life of the older sister.

Another time, Lorraine followed me out to the "little house behind the house." She forgot to fasten the gate, and again Buck followed her and she came running toward me. I opened the door to the outhouse far enough for her to get in but she was going so fast that she went around the corner instead. Around and around they went, again and again.

Finally she got far enough ahead of Buck that she was able to squeeze in with me. We were both trapped in that sweetly-perfumed prison until Buck lost interest. Then we sneaked out into the yard and made sure the gate was securely fastened. That left Buck out in the main yard for Dad to cope with.

Again, my fault. Oh well, such is life and by that time I was used to it and took it for granted.

Buck continued his bunting ways for several more years until, one day, in late summer, when Dad was sitting on the ground at the rear of the single row corn picker, getting ready for corn harvest in the fall. Buck decided that Dad's head was a good target. After Dad got his bloodied face untangled from the gears he was working on, he took after that stupid animal. Even the wrench Dad used to bean him with only made Buck shake his head.

Soon after that Buck was off to the sale barn. He had worn out his welcome and his usefulness. He was replaced with a more docile breeding animal before it was time for the rams to go to work again in the fall. The exchange happened on the same day in the same sale barn. My father was happy with the new resident in our sheepfold but I often wondered how pleased the new owner was with his Bunting Buck.

Author **Delores (Philiph) Swanson** was married to a farmer, J. Oscar Swanson, for 55 years. They lived on a farm near May City most of their married life and raised sheep most of those years. They had four children, two boys and two girls. After they retired they lived on an acreage and Delores had a flock of 50 ewes, for which she did all the lambing and necessary work. The family all agrees that the farm is a great place to raise a family.

Photo provided by Delores Swanson

Photo provided b H. "Bumper" Bauer

OF OLD DOGS AND MEN

H. "Bumper" Bauer

Last evening, while sitting in my chair reading a book, I noticed that Murphy, my Golden Retriever who was on the couch, was obviously immersed in one heck of a dream. His now-white muzzle was twitching and his paws were flicking up and down as if involved in a great chase. He was plainly enjoying whatever it was that he was dreaming about, because once in a while the very end of his tail would twitch just a bit and he would emit a low, bubbling little howl.

Watching his actions made me think about how much we were truly alike, both of us now only remembering our best hunts in our dreams.

Throughout our many years together we have enjoyed the pursuit of game. We had loved nothing better than being in grapevine-shrouded thickets or endless fields of corn on a frosty fall morning, Murphy looking for a scent to follow and I loving everything God had sent immersed in the vibrant colors of the leaves, the musky, wine-like scent of the woods, and the soft crunch of frost-covered leaves beneath my feet as I walk behind the dog that's dancing out in front of me.

Then there were the unexpected surprises, when a sudden cackle or whirr of wings as a pheasant or grouse suddenly takes to the sky. An extraordinary moment in time that we both instantly react to by shifting into actions bred into us by years of hunting together. My part being the shot and kill, and his to retrieve, both accomplished without thinking, in well-tuned harmony.

As I settled back into my chair, Murphy opened his eyes in a half-dream state, glanced at me for a split second then closed them again, returning to his special place to continue his dream.

The instant I saw the way his deep brown eyes were looking at me, I remembered that identical look in someone else's eyes long ago. That immediate recognition of a companion or loved one, which conveys a message that everything is OK. I had seen that look in the eyes of my grandfather when I'd visited him just prior to his passing.

When I'd arrived at the farm that morning, Pap was upstairs in a little room at the side of the house that he used as a den and bedroom, due to failing health. He'd chosen the room because it was filled with windows and he could sit in his rocking chair and look out on the farm where he had lived and worked for more than fifty years.

Pap was absorbed in cleaning his old, A.H. Fox 16-gauge side-by-side, which I knew he had not used in many years. As I neared the doorway I noticed he had a faraway look in his eyes and I wondered if he was reliving a moment from his past, perhaps a special day when he had used that shotgun. I stood silently watching as he tucked the stock of the gun against his weathered cheek, sighting down the barrels toward a target known only to him. I wondered what he was thinking at that moment.

He lowered the gun, then slowly began rubbing fine linseed oil into its stock with a piece of tattered chamois that certainly had seen as many days as him. With every gentle stoke of the cloth, I felt he was being taken farther and farther back to when he was young and had the ability to run his beloved fields and mountains of Pennsylvania endlessly.

As I stepped slowly into the room, Tillie, Pap's old beagle, lifted her head from the floor where she had been sleeping next to his rocking chair. Both of them accepted my arrival, Pap with a broad smile and Tillie with a slight wag of her tail and a muted groan.

Someone once said that the eyes are the windows to the soul. I am a firm believer of that statement.

Pap always insisted that dogs had more sense than humans, and I have to say at this point in my life I agree with him. A dog asks for little more than a warm bed, food to eat, clean water to drink, and an occasional pat on the head. It's astounding what they give in return: unquestioning love and devotion.

A man who has reached the autumn of his life is much like an old dog. He does not require or ask for more. A little love and attention is the one thing that makes both most happy. A simple pat on the head for the dog, and someone's lending a willing ear to the man, in most cases, is enough to make his day.

Much can and will be learned from both by the young among us if they would take the time and care enough to watch and listen. The old dog and old man have in their time learned to hunt and outfox, through experience, the most cunning of game. Any good breeder or trainer of dogs will be the first to tell you that when you put a young pup with an older experienced dog, the pup will quickly learn from it, cutting the training time in half. It's not much different with an old man and a young man. If a young man is perceptive enough to listen to what that old guy has to say, he too will become a better hunter in half the time.

The old dog and man have learned from years of practice in the field and through trial and error what works and what will not. Don't sidestep either or take them for granted, for there is a wealth of knowledge to be gained from both of them.

Do it now, before you wake up one day and hear yourself saying I wish I would have or should have! I can't count the times since Pap's passing that, without thinking, I reach for the phone to tell him about something good that has happened or ask his advice about a problem. How many times have you told your aging dog and best buddy to scat when he was bothersome?

There will come a day all too soon when you will wish he was there, being a pest. Nothing would make me feel better than to be able to scratch those velvet ears of my long gone beagle Mike just one more time. But he's gone now, as is Pap.

We're alike, my old dog and I, and I wouldn't have it any other way.

Hunt Hard, Hunt Safe and Hunt Fair

H. "Bumper" Bauer is an award-winning freelance writer and wildlife photographer from Brookville, Pa.

Photo provided by Terry Overocker

NO PETS ALLOWED

Terry Overocker

Growing up on a farm gave me a sense of love and compassion for animals. Feeding and caring for livestock and family pets were the chores given to kids too young to be working in the fields. The cattle, horses, cats, kittens and dogs were my responsibility. Getting food and water to each animal could be a chore at times, but loving them was not. To me, they were family.

After being outdoors with the cats and dogs all day I wanted to bring them into the house at night. But many farmers, including my parents, were of the mentality that animals belonged outside. No pets were allowed in the house. That meant a lot of creativity and secrecy were needed to get my pets inside. I couldn't understand my parents reasoning for not wanting animals in the house, and to this day they are unaware of all the times we had cats, kittens, dogs, rabbits, birds and turtles in our home.

Saturday was the day my parents were usually busy shopping and doing errands away from the farm. I often had the house to myself because my sisters were involved in sports and activities with friends. My passions were my pets and playing the piano. I practiced the piano all week, and since I had received a typewriter for Christmas I typed up concert programs on Friday nights. As soon as everyone was gone on Saturday, I brought many of my pets into the music room and entertained them with a piano recital.

It was difficult at times, when they walked up and down the piano keyboard and wandered all over the house. After I found a kitten asleep in my bed one Saturday night I decided it might be better to play for my stuffed animals. If my parents ever found any pets that I hadn't gotten out of the house, I would have been in big trouble.

My stuffed animals, on the other hand, were a captivated audience. I escorted them to the music room, gave them each a program and none of them wandered off. At the end of the concert they applauded and cheered loudly, and always requested an encore. They were an appreciative audience. The outdoor pets had second thoughts about their poor behavior when they found themselves outside, looking in the screen door. The next week they were invited back in with my stuffed animals, and for a while they behaved a little better.

As an adult, my own home has always been blessed with pets. They are my children. My pets have brought so much comfort and joy into my life. They are an endless source of entertainment and laughter.

Some of my friends who once lived on a farm still prefer animals to be outside. Whenever my best friend Rita and her husband Paul are at my home, my pets make it their duty to win them over. Rita and Paul didn't dislike animals—they just preferred them to be outdoors.

Animals seem to have a sixth sense if someone is not overly fond of them and they often choose to go to that person. Sammy, my yellow lab, will sit as close to Paul as she can get, which is almost on his lap, and stare at him with big, brown adoring eyes. My cats, Caleb, Jackson and Noah, surround Rita. Jackson reaches out with his paws and constantly pokes her while meowing and purring loudly.

"Why are they doing that?" Rita asked.

"They like you," I replied.

Rita and Paul had no pets of their own. Until Kitty showed up at their door.

At first they tried to ignore her, but every day she was there so they finally had to feed her. Soon there was a cat dish on their porch. Then a box with a blanket for a bed, and even a two-story carpeted cat condo appeared. Rita asked me what kind of brush I used on my cats and was concerned that the brushes in the stores seemed too hard.

Kitty really knew what she was doing. Paul built her a ledge beneath the kitchen window so she could sit and watch them in the house. When the weather turned colder Paul's shop became a heated winter home for Kitty. But Rita and Paul missed not having Kitty at the door as much, so soon Kitty was spending the days in the house with Rita.

As the snow got deeper, Paul carried Kitty back and forth from the shop to the house so her feet would not get cold. Then a bed and a scratching pole appeared in the house. Kitty trained them well. She stood at the door and meowed when she wanted out and she stood at the door and meowed when she wanted in.

One night Paul was up several times checking to see if Kitty was at the door, but the weather was warmer and Kitty liked staying outdoors. When she didn't come home for a couple of days, Rita went to the humane society to see if kitty might have ended up there. Kitty was back at the door after a few days. Rita and Paul talked about taking her to the vet to be spayed but thought that if she had a litter of kittens she would be happier.

Rita and Paul and Kitty are now the proud parents of four beautiful black kittens. Paul's shop has become a kitty play-land, and he converted a window into a cat door so Kitty can come and go as she pleases. Kitty has five food dishes with a buffet of food choices because she is eating for five now.

Paul and Rita spend their evenings in the shop while their family provides hours of entertainment.

Terry Overocker lives in a log cabin on the family farm where she grew up. She loves gardening and grows and preserves most of the year's food. She also enjoys music, reading, hiking, writing and caring for her family of cats and a yellow Lab named Sammy.

Photo provided by Arlene Walker

DAD AND THE CHRISTMAS OPOSSUM

Mark Smith

Whenever our family meets, the children come to me and ask what it was like to grow up on a farm. I tell them it was boring and a lot of work and try to go back to my coffee. But, led by my daughter, they clamor until I reluctantly toss some tidbit out.

Take, for instance, that Christmas Eve, 1968, when Dad found a 'possum.

In the summer time we boys loved the barn. We had dirt-clod fights in the haymow. We climbed to the rafters to try to catch the pigeons that flew in and out through the windows. We jumped on the lumber pile, bouncing on the planks like a trampoline. But winter was different. In winter the barn became darker, colder, spookier and smellier than in other months.

As Dad headed out to feed and water the animals that particular time, he turned off the TV and announced that he wasn't going to do all the work by himself. Dad hated TV. He felt it wasted time better spent doing other things—like working.

My brothers had prepared for this moment by producing homework, but I hadn't thought ahead. As I put on my coat and boots, I knew that the TV would be back on before Dad and I even got to the barn. But there was no use complaining.

Once in the barn, I scooped oats with one hand while holding my flashlight in the other. That's when I saw it: a hairless tail more than a foot long, sticking out between some boards.

"Dad," I hollered. "There's a giant rat down here!"

"There's no such thing as a giant rat," he called back to me. "Finish feeding the horses."

"But I can see it."

As Dad climbed down from the haymow I could hear him growling to himself. I couldn't make out all the words, but I'm pretty sure I heard ". . . kids and their crazy imaginations."

I watched the tail in mounting horror, now afraid that it would disappear before Dad got here. He finally arrived, but I wasn't prepared for what happened next.

Dad looked at the enormous tail for a moment, then reached down, grabbed it and pulled. Holding the struggling animal at an arm's length, he said, "Let's go to the house."

As soon as we got inside the back porch, Dad hollered for Mom to come and to bring my brothers with her.

When everyone had arrived, he proudly held up the squirming creature, still firmly held by the tail, and announced, "Boys, this is an opossum."

Like I said, Dad hated TV, but there was one show that he never missed: *Mutual of Omaha's Wild Kingdom*. Dad loved to watch as Marlin Perkins traveled to remote places to capture unusual animals. He would sit transfixed as Marlin Perkins reached into a hollow tree and dragged out a ring-tailed bandicoot . . . or whatever.

In later years, when Marlin got a little past confronting the wild, Jim Fowler was hired to do the rough stuff while Marlin commented in a voice over: *"As you can see, Jim is wrestling with a Komodo dragon, trying to stuff it into the crate to be shipped to . . . Oh, Jim should not have let it bite him. Now we will have to disinfect the wound because the Komodo dragon has dangerous bacteria in its mouth . . ."*

Dad was in his glory as he explained the intricacies of 'possum psychology. "The opossum, when frightened, faints and appears to be dead. This is where we get the phrase 'playing 'possum.'"

While Dad was talking, the opossum stopped flailing and starting rocking back and forth. Dad banged the opossum against the wall to demonstrate its "natural defenses." But instead of fainting, the animal grabbed its tail with one paw.

"Ahh, Dad," I said.

"Not now, son. You see, dogs and other creatures won't touch a dead animal. So the . . ."

Normally I would have pointed out that our dog regularly dragged dead animals to the front porch, but I was more concerned with the fact that the *live* animal in Dad's hand had just grabbed its tail with the other front paw as well.

"Dad . . ."

"Dammit, it boy, I'm trying to teach you something here."

By now my brothers had noticed the upward movement of the captive opossum as it continued to climb paw-over-paw up its tail toward the hand that was holding it. They began jumping up and down, shouting and trying to warn Dad.

The opossum pulled itself up and bit Dad's hand.

Dad yelled one of those words that Mom didn't want us to know about and tossed the opossum out the back door. If possum pitching were an Olympic event, Dad would have won a gold medal. It flew twenty yards before it hit the first snow bank, skipped another ten feet to a second one, then hit a third snow bank and spun to a complete stop, where it lay still on top of the snow.

"You did it, Dad!" we shouted excitedly. "The 'possum fainted."

Dad said a few more words and went to wash and bandage his hand.

The next morning, Christmas Day, before a single present was opened, we went outside to check the snow bank. The opossum was gone.

"Dad sure knows a lot about 'possums," one of my brothers said as he reached for one of the blueberry muffins Mom always made for Christmas breakfast.

"He sure does," my other brother agreed. "But what did that word he said when it bit him mean?"

"It means," Mom said, "that the next time he finds an opossum in the barn, he's going to leave it there!"

Mark Smith says, "In the mid '60s, our dad decided he didn't like the way the neighborhood was going, so he bought a dilapidated farm and raised us the way he would have liked to have been raised." The resulting childhood of adventures involving work, livestock, hunting and simple pleasures with firearms and the occasional explosion, would cause modern social workers' heads to spin off their shoulders if told, but alas, will never win him a spot on Oprah.

MAMA AND THE RATTLESNAKE

Ed Stevens

Our old Ford was of a bizarre hue—an insipid amalgam of rust, mud and bird droppings. The upholstery had endured too many downpours with open windows, and even on the driest days of deep summer it bore a dampish, mildewed odor, not unlike an aging wharf—not exactly fishy but certainly not sunny "Nebraska wheat field" either.

It rattled and clunked and emitted steam, smoke and less readily identifiable vapors from a dozen cracks and crevices. It had spoked wheels, a spare tire centrally mounted just above the rear bumper and a hood ornament that was a miniature mostly-nude woman with wings, holding an automobile tire and facing bravely into onrushing winds. This chrome lady had originally decorated the prow of Chauncey Pettigrew's Packard, but had come to live on our battered Ford one night after a particularly spirited game of cribbage between Chauncey and my dad.

Everyone in the family more or less hated the car but grudgingly granted that it was slightly better than walking, especially when we had to haul the family laundry to Grandma's house to use her chugging Maytag washer—a luxury we aspired to but had not yet attained.

And laundry was our mission on that particular day. Two wooden baskets brimming with soiled socks, overalls and unmentionables roosted serenely on the back seat. My sister Sherilyn and I poked and elbowed each other in the passenger side of the front seat; Mama scolded our quibblings as she simultaneously wrestled with the old car's controls.

Suddenly, she slammed the brakes hard. Tires skidded, dust plumed, and Sherilyn and I banged smartly into the dashboard. Both laundry baskets came to rest upside down on the rear floorboards, their contents strewn unceremoniously through the nether regions of the Ford.

"Darn, I missed him!" Mama snorted, then threw the gearshift into reverse and poked her bandana'd head out the window to peer anxiously to the rear as we backed several yards up the road.

A fat gray rattlesnake had been crossing the rutted dirt road and Mama had attempted to employ the infamous "slide" technique to liquidate him. It's well known among country folk that you cannot kill a snake simply by running over it, especially one as big as this one. A successful "slide" called for applying the brakes at the precise moment the tire was on the snake, with the resulting skid thereby abrading and contusing him sufficiently to end his scaly existence.

Sadly, the slide maneuver requires split-second timing and the reflexes of an Olympic gymnast, both attributes notably lacking in my mother. The big reptile had managed to elude the skidding tires and had made his way safely into the ditch where he was now menacingly coiled—mad as a hornet and buzzing like a pair of maracas. He glared up at us, his slitted snaky eyes burning, his black tongue flicking in and out.

Now, in my part of the country there are certain things that simply aren't done—you don't squat with your spurs on, you don't drink downstream from the herd, and you never, ever willingly allow a rattler to escape unscathed. Mama knew this as she sat slumped over the steering wheel of the idling Ford, mulling her options.

Undiscouraged by her failure to skid the snake into the hereafter, she suddenly dived into the toolbox my father always carried in the car for unexpected road repairs, and began hauling out various tools. Carefully selected by their propensity to be large, heavy, and made of iron, she began heaving them at the snake. First went the jack handle, followed by a ball-peen hammer, a pair of fence pliers, two large mill files and a rusty Stillson wrench.

Her armamentarium exhausted, mama stood on the running board of the Ford and squinted into the ditch to evaluate the effects of her barrage. To her consternation, she found that all her missiles had either missed or bounced harmlessly off the rattling reptile—no damage at all had been inflicted upon his slithery corpus, but he was now *seriously* annoyed. The upside was that we had discovered several weighty metallic items that are of distinctly limited utility when killing large snakes.

Swell . . . now we had an enraged rattlesnake, still very much alive, and in sole possession of most of the contents of Dad's toolbox. The situation had taken on the essential character of what in the Sand Hills is known as a Mexican standoff. But Mama was stubbornly resourceful and, after a moment's reflection, dispatched Sherilyn down the road to the McCarty place—about a half-mile away—with instructions to grab one of the McCarty boys and his gun and come a-running.

I watched Sherilyn tentatively step off down that dry road, barefoot and frightened, little puffs of dust squirting up between her sun-browned toes. Every few steps she would glance uneasily over her shoulder to be sure that the snake wasn't mounting a covert assault from the rear.

As my nervous sister grew smaller in the distance, Mama and I kept the snake's attention by pelting him periodically with small clods of dirt cadged from the side of the road. We wanted to be sure he didn't tire of guarding his newly acquired cache of tools and decide to crawl away to a calmer setting. After nearly half an hour and about a million clods, Sherilyn arrived back at the scene of the siege with Robby, who at 14 was the youngest of the McCarty boys.

With his twelve gauge shotgun in hand, Robby peered manfully into the weedy ditch for a few seconds and then sent two loads of buckshot crashing into our nemesis—thus summarily ending the Great Snake Stand-off.

After he'd given the snake both barrels, Mama borrowed his Barlow jack knife and scrambled into the ditch, emerging a minute or two later triumphantly brandishing a bloody skein of nine rattles. A second trip into the ditch fetched all the tools, after which everyone milled about for a few moments, laughing and chattering with relief at having witnessed the dragon slain.

Finally, Mama, with a last baleful glance at the shattered remains of the snake, herded everyone into the car. As we drove away, the Saga of the Rattlesnake morphed almost imperceptibly from current to past family lore status. Routine reasserted itself as we rumbled dustily down the road, pausing only to drop Robby off at his mailbox, then continuing on to Grandma's to tend to the laundry.

Mama, Dad and Sherilyn are all gone now, but sometimes on a hot summer night, when the whirring of the cicadas crowds my senses and holds sleep at bay, I will root around in my store of memories to once more savor that long ago afternoon . . . with Mama and the Rattlesnake.

Ed Stevens is a native Nebraskan, retiree-cum geezer and now spends his days as a purveyor of used books—a completely delightful pursuit, by the way. He writes short stories, a blog, a bit of poetry, and has recently become interested in memoir as a robust literary form. He values his family, his country and his dignity—in that order.

Photo provided by C. R. Lindemer

COMING THROUGH, WILMA!

By C. R. Lindemer

In the 1960s, our Holstein cattle were still roaming in a grassy pasture bordered by a row of mountain ash trees. Our barn was a typical massive, white wooden dairy barn with a huge second-level loft—pierced with a hay elevator to the third story—always looking a little "tired" in places.

Every morning at 6:00 a.m., and repeating again around 6:00 p.m., my dad would call the cows to come in to be milked.

"Come Boss, Come Boss!" he would yell a few times, and then wait a few seconds. "Come Boss, Come Boss!" he'd yell once again.

Once he got their attention, all of the black-and-white spotted cows would slowly lumber, side-to-side, single file, down the worn and winding path to the back of the barn. Once inside, they all knew exactly where to go. There were 24 milking stalls, and each cow stepped into her special place to the left or to the right.

As a young girl, and having no brothers, one of my early morning chores was to feed the cows as they were waiting to be milked. I often did this before catching the school bus.

After climbing up a silo ladder through a corrugated vertical metal tube, I shoveled warm silage down to a wheelbarrow resting many feet below. After breaking through the dried outer crust, the moist warm silage steamed up in the icy Minnesota air, the pungent aroma of souring corn, sliced and diced corncobs, and fermenting chopped cornstalks rose in smoky grey puffs with each fermenting forkful. I shoveled the silage through the square opening and kept checking the slowly filling wheelbarrow below.

I'd then crawl through the opening and climb down the ladder to deliver warm breakfasts to dozens of cows in a long cement trough. They all munched their silage as their individual stanchions were closed, metal scraping against rusting metal, around their solid necks as the stanchions were all latched by hand with twenty-four raspy *clangs.*

Every cow in the herd had a short name because of the dairy production system that hauled our Grade A milk. No name could be longer than six letters. Elsie, Fern, Gert, Iris, Jewel, Luella, Nan, Roxie, and Selma were typical cow names on our farm. The names seemed old-fashioned to me at the time. My parents had named them all.

There was one place in the barn where a cow could swing her body over and stand blocking the path to the silo. When that happened we would yell, "Coming through!" give that cow a little whack on the hip, and wait for her to saunter over.

For many years, the cow next to that path was my personal cow, named "Wilma." We all yelled, "Coming through, Wilma!" on a regular basis for many years. Wilma would take her time, but she would always kindly step to the side to let us through.

Sometimes Dad, after removing a dripping milking machine, would squirt milk from a cow's teat to the cats that gathered in the milking barn. He would get a cat standing up on its hind feet and we'd watch it tiptoeing backwards, doing a little side-step as it tried to catch a mouthful of milk. That was Dad's little "farming humor," and it made us laugh. The cats got pretty messy after their little warm, sprayed drinks.

I had many chores for our Holstein calves and the cows. Mixing powdered calf milk replacer with warm water for newly weaned calves was one of them. I "tasted" the fine milk powder as I scooped it from the chain-stitched paper bag while breathing in. It was sweet, and it wasn't all that bad, especially before my breakfast.

In the winter mornings before school, thawing frozen water pipes with lukewarm water was sometimes necessary. And a lot of times I'd clean up the walkway during milking times with a wide shovel, scraping the slippery splattered "cow pies" which had landed in the center walkway into two foot-deep cement gutters running the length of the barn. I got used to the smell of cow manure, and it rarely bothered me.

We spent a lot of time—hours every day—hanging out and working in our dairy barn. I remember once seeing my dad doing push-ups in front of the cows, against the whitewashed barn wall, while the milking machines worked away with that regular, rhythmic *pump-a-pump, pump-a-pump* cadence. Dad was young and fit back then and had the energy for brief workouts, even with all of the work of running a dairy farm.

One summer day at lunchtime my family and I were all sitting at our kitchen table with our heads soberly bowed to say grace. It was my turn to say the blessing. And instead of saying our usual common prayer which began with "Come, Lord Jesus," for some odd reason, or force of habit, I started my prayer with the words "Coming through, Wilma!"

We all burst out laughing, and it was hopeless to continue. It was a family joke for years.

C.R. Lindemer writes stories, poems, and essays at her historic farmstead in New England. She is the editor of *True Cow Tales: Literary Sketches and Stories by Farmers, Ranchers, and Dairy Princesses* and has written a children's picture book (Shapato Publishing). She has lived in Massachusetts for more than twenty years but never lost her Minnesota accent.

Photo provided by R. C. Davis

CANE POLE LOGIC

R. C. Davis

I had been wandering the small eastern Iowa town for hours. My family had moved in not more then a week before and I was enamored with all that it was. Earlier that morning I had been standing in the tiny Standard station at the town square, drinking a bottle of Nesbitt's orange soda that I had pulled from the mammoth, red lift-top machine. A "water bath slider," they called it. You had to herd your choice of bottles through a maze of metal dividers to a common hold before you could claim your ten ounce prize with the drop of a dime—an ingenious design.

The sun, peeking over the silent tavern across the street, bathed me in its warmth as I lingered in the open front door and listened to the locals chat. The focus of the populace always seemed to be on the Wapsipinicon, a small river that flowed through the center of the town.

Lively discussions ensued about boating and fishing, who had caught what kind of fish and how big it was. Tales of monster catfish, sleek northern pike and the value of one bluegill versus a pan full. The exchange always seemed to end with stories about "the one that got away."

After about an hour's worth of "hot air," there would be a lull while the aged orators caught their breath; then it would start all over again.

It was 1968 and the nation was in turmoil. The Vietnam conflict was wrecking havoc on America, and lines were being drawn in the sand. As a twelve-year-old boy, it hadn't yet touched me. The innocence of youth still shielded me and ignorance brought me a bliss that I have not felt since.

I was up at dawn so I would have the entire day to survey the neighborhoods. I walked the tree-lined streets and ogled the huge old houses. Birdsong was in abundance and the air was filled with all kinds of smells. Bacon wafted from an open window as I cut through the dew-laden grass of someone's backyard, the aroma of the lilacs and flowering crab trees competed, and then there was the smell of the river. I can only describe that as an odor of decaying vegetation, but it was like cologne to me. It drew me like a bee to a flower. It rode the breeze into my bedroom window at night and tried to lure me from my bed. I couldn't get enough of it.

Strolling down the street that paralleled my beloved waterway, I turned away and ventured up a hill into a newer section. I soon grew tired from my walk up the steep grade and sat down on a curb, my back against a signpost. However, I'd no more than become comfortable when I caught a whiff of fish and looked about to locate the source.

Across the street and two houses up from me, it sat. A squat, beige clapboard building covering at least a third of the block, with a large white sign at least sixteen feet in length hanging at the roof line. Its red letters proclaimed Lucky's Live Bait and Fishing Equipment.

I stood up and ran, my lethargy vanishing. Stopping on the concrete apron at the front, I felt I had died and gone to heaven—the Pearly Gates were presented to me in the form of two wooden screen doors that opened at the center.

The air was filled with the sound of a huge, rusty white cooler that rested just outside the door. A paper sign taped to its side read: "Night Crawlers, 10 Cents a Dozen!" as if we should all be excited that Lucky was graciously dispensing such a valuable commodity at such a remarkable price.

I strolled up to the doors and peered in through the mesh.

From what I could see, it appeared a paradise. There were great bubbling aquariums arranged in a row at the center. Display rack after display rack lined the walls with a million lures of all kinds and functions. Fishhooks, nets and cartons of liver bait filled the shelves. Hip and bib waders hung from the ceiling in the back corner along with a brand new wooden canoe.

I pulled one of the doors open. The hinges squeaked and the rusty spring screamed its disapproval. Stepping inside, I let the door slam shut.

"What ye wont?" rolled across the room like thunder as an old man stood up behind the glass-fronted counter.

I cringed and turned to the door to flee—then froze as my eyes fell upon the fishing poles sequestered on the wall next to the entryway.

"I've come for a pole" I stuttered out, my apprehension apparent. I was shaken, and a little boy's guilt invaded my body as though I'd done something terribly wrong.

"Well, there they are, young fella." He pointed with his cane at the rack.

Taking my hand off of the door handle, I took a deep breath, calmed myself, turned back to the man and smiled. "Thanks" I squeaked.

I stared across the space at his thick glasses and greasy grey hair. He was a big man with an even bigger belly. I imagined him having swallowed a whole watermelon without having chewed any of it. Realizing that I was staring I quickly looked back at the poles.

He started to say something then changed his mind. Sitting down, he turned his attention back to his newspaper, holding it just low enough to see over the top. I supposed just so he could keep an eye on me in the case I should snatch up a can of O'Brian's Dough Ball Bait and make a run for it.

Focusing on the rack before me, I scanned it from end to end. It must have been a good twenty-five feet long at the least, running from door to counter. It held every kind of fishing pole known to man: spring-steel poles, fiberglass poles, old-fashioned wooden poles that pulled apart for convenient transport, and right in the middle of the display were the ten-foot-long cane poles.

A strange feeling came over me as I looked at those cherry brown beauties, a feeling that I can only describe now as love.

The dim light from the ceiling fixtures gleamed off of their varnished shafts and reflected off the large silver eyelets that had been affixed to the small end of each cane. Tied to that was a heavy cotton line that ran almost its entire length. Stopping just short of the opposite end, it looped through a tiny clasp protruding from the side. It then returned to the tip where it was attached with a large gold-colored fishhook. This gave the user almost twenty feet of line to toss into their favorite fishing hole. Then my eye fell upon the little device known as the bobber.

Strung about a foot from that magnificent fishhook, the bobber in itself was a piece of work, a beautiful thing that caught the eye of young boys and made them marvel as women did at diamonds.

This one was made of balsa wood and painted white; slender green, blue and red stripes ran around its bulbous middle that was skewered by a three-inch wooden dowel. I reached out and ran a finger along one of the poles. It was smooth and cool to my touch.

"Three-fifty and its yers, kid"

I stole a glance at the old man, who was now smiling. I looked down at the index card thumb-tacked to the bottom of the rack below the poles: "$3.50! Reduced from $5, a Real Bargain!" it declared in red and black marker.

I turned my back to the man and reached into the pockets of my cutoff jeans. I pulled out three wrinkled one dollar bills, two dimes, six pennies and a marble, a beautiful aggie that I cherished. Additional contents were assorted bits of lint, a stick of Black Jack gum and an old brass skeleton key that I'd found in our landlady's garage.

Turning back I said, "I don't have enough."

I gave him a look of despair and shrugged.

He stood up. A grimace crossed his face for a second. "Damn that hurts," he growled.

He hobbled around the counter, his wooden cane clacking on the oily boards of the floor at every other step. He rocked up and down as he came.

I could see that walking was a painful task for him, and his actions frightened me for some reason. It took a degree of self-control to keep from backing away. I stood my ground, though, as he approached.

When he arrived he clamped his stick in his armpit and said in a kindly manner, "How much ye got thar, little fella?" Bending down, he reached out and cupped my hands in his so he could count.

"I'll take those thar dollars and that thar stick of gum and, let's see . . ." Reaching out, he grabbed the best-looking cane pole of the lot. "Ye can have this one har, it's a goodun! Howz bout it, do we have a deal?"

"Are you sure? I mean are you serious? The sign says it was five dollars once!"

"Why of carse I'm sure, sonny. That's wot I call 'Cane Pole Logic' and besides, I'm the boss har!" He cackled at that and his watermelon belly jiggled.

I was consumed by elation. Looking up I said, my voice cracked with excitement, "Okay mister, you got a deal!"

He reached into my hands with his free one and carefully picked out all of the paper money and the gum.

"You can call me Lucky," he said proudly as he pushed the pole toward me.

I shoved the coins and other possessions into my pockets and then gingerly reached out and wrapped my fingers around the bamboo shaft.

"Grab yerself a carton of them warms out front while yer at it, but take it from the front, thar the oldest!"

I mustered a, "Thanks Lucky!" and slipped through the front doors. I reached into the cooler and grabbed one of the waxed, cardboard cartons.

I left at a fast walk and as soon as I cleared the corner of the building I started to run. It was kind of a skipping run, and down the hill I went. Halfway to the bottom of the hill the river came into view and at this distance I could see leaves floating on its surface and dirty foam swirling around the rocks where the old bridge used to be.

As I bounced down the street, I carried the cane pole in my left hand, the tip well above my head. The rays of the sun played through the leaves of the trees and glinted off that beautiful gold fishhook.

I slowed to a walk when the fragrance of the river reached my nose, and I just couldn't stop smiling.

A world traveler with a deep-seated love for the works of Mark Twain, author **R. C. Davis** has been writing poetry and prose since his twelfth year. He resides in Fairfax, Iowa, with his wife Anne and their two dogs.

Photo provided by Gene Miller

WHAT'S IN A NAME?

Gene Miller

Peanie, Beanie, Dick and Slim. Shorty, Gomer, Honkey and Bud. Irish, Duck, Puggy, Gus and Fritz.

Everybody in town called them by their nicknames, so it wasn't until I was an adult that I learned these men had real names. Names like Hugo, Bernard, Richard, Clarence, Walter, Tom, Merwin, Harlan, Woodrow, Lorenze and Jesse.

To be raised in or near Lone Rock, Iowa, in the 1950s, '60s and early '70s was to be raised in a fishbowl. The proverbial fishbowl, but a fishbowl nonetheless.

We all knew each other and knew *about* each other and for the most part cared about one another. Although some might consider it stifling and restricting I found it a grand place to grow up. To use current popular vernacular, I was raised by the village despite the fact that I actually grew up on a farm one mile east of town.

It's said that familiarity breeds contempt, but I personally can attest to the fact that it can also breed fun. There are some things you can only say to a stranger, but there are some things you can only say to those who know you well, and vice versa. You say these things to them and they intuitively know what and whom you're talking about.

Some would call it gossip. But that, too, can be a misnomer. Or, as the old saying goes, "We don't gossip about our neighbors. The things we say are true."

The men I speak of, and they were all men, as I remember no women with nicknames, did a variety of things to make a living. They were farmers, blacksmiths, truck drivers, construction workers and local merchants. They were young, middle-aged and elderly. Some were married and some were not. Some had children and some did not. Some were brothers. Some were father and son. All in all, they were a colorful set of characters and as a child I remember being both

135

amused and intimidated by them all at the same time. Most of them are now deceased.

Honkey was a practical joker. Slim had a voice that could wake the dead, while Dick at times was barely audible. Gus was known for his common sense. Puggy liked to cuss, especially when our local pastor was around, which he, our pastor, took in stride as you need to do when living in a small town.

But of all of these men, the one who was the most mysterious was the one nicknamed Peanie.

In my family we rarely went into the town pool hall. It just wasn't who we were. But on the rare occasion that we did I would inevitably see Peanie perched on a barstool at the west end of the bar, drinking beer. Not one beer, mind you, but beer after beer after beer.

Some people in Lone Rock in those days referred to Peanie as the "town drunk" or the "town lush." Phrases that today would be incredibly politically incorrect, but in those days were entirely acceptable. This was, after all, the era of *The Andy Griffith Show* on television and, though I exaggerate, it seemed as if every small town in American had its very own Otis Campbell, the man who drank too much on a regular basis but whose safety was seen after by all of the local residents. Otis didn't have to worry about getting run over by a car in Mayberry and neither did Peanie in Lone Rock.

Peanie, whose real name was Hugo, lived only a block from the pool hall. He lived with his mother, Lillian, in a small, two-story green-sided house that she had occupied since 1900. It was located on the north end of Lone Rock's Main Street, where the businesses stopped and the residential area began.

He did odd jobs for local businessmen and farmers, and he helped his mother around the house. And he went to the bar on a nightly basis. Never once did I see him in church or at a school function. I did see him, from time to time, however, at American Legion events, which may have been in part because he was a veteran. But with the exception of the pool hall, Peanie, for the most part, kept to himself.

I also remember him being a man of opinions. They weren't always informed opinions. I recognized this even as a child, but they were opinions nonetheless, and once he had enough beers under his belt he wasn't afraid to share them with anyone who would listen.

People sometimes laughed at him behind his back. Sometimes to his face, though it wasn't as malicious as it may sound. It was simply the way he was treated, had come to expect to be treated, and in some ways encouraged the treatment as he himself could exhibit a rather gruff demeanor with others.

He was what he was—someone who drank too much, couldn't hold a regular job, lived with mother and had a life that didn't seem to amount to a lot.

I left Lone Rock more than thirty-five years ago but would go back from time to time to see my parents, my siblings or a friend or two. I pretty much forgot about Peanie. He had simply become another childhood memory.

Peanie died in 1981, a few years after his mother. Between the two of them they'd been practically destitute. In the end he had no money, few living relatives, little other than the small, raggedy house on the corner. The funeral was a government-funded Title IXX affair. In order to recoup some of the cost, the local funeral director had the house leveled and sold the lot upon which it had sat.

For reasons I have never been fully able to comprehend or articulate . . . I bought the lot.

It was at this point that I learned something about Peanie that I'd never before known. As I've asked around town, I haven't found anyone else who knew it either. I even asked my mother, who has lived in Lone Rock all of her life.

People knew Peanie had grown up around Lone Rock. They knew he was one of seven children: Enos, Josie, Sylvia, Lillian, Edith, Hulda and Hug. They knew that as a young man during World War II he had been gone for a few years of military service, like most other young men his age. They also knew that about a year or two after the war had ended he'd returned to Lone Rock, moved in with his mother and began the pattern of life that I have already described.

That was pretty much all they knew. So what I learned after I received the Warranty Deed on his mother's property surprised nearly everyone.

Peanie had actually at one point in his life been married. He was also the father of three children, now grown and all living near Fayetteville, West Virginia. Apparently there had been a divorce, and afterwards Peanie had sought refuge in Lone Rock. In other words, he simply came home.

But in all the years Peanie rambled about the streets of Lone Rock, no one had ever heard him say a word about a wife, three children or a failed marriage. He hadn't even talked about it when sober.

Many times since I first read the Warranty Deed to that little lot in Lone Rock I've thought about the man I knew as Peanie. I've wondered about the anguish he must have known. About the pain he might have felt. Pain buried so deep that none of us, for more than thirty-five years, ever truly saw it. All we saw was the balding, pear-shaped lump of a man sitting at the end of the bar, locked in his own self-imposed prison. And I am no longer convinced that alcohol was the only cause of that faraway look in his eye.

I would imagine that many a night Hugo Worthington sat on his stool at the east end of the bar in the pool hall in Lone Rock, Iowa, and thought about his children and wondered what they were doing and how there were getting along. And he probably never quite got over what had happened, but he got on with life because what else is there to do?

So he came home to Lone Rock. In all likelihood did the best he could, and became our Peanie.

It would be tempting to try to say something profound, but what is there really to be said? Life is sometimes tragic. Life is sometimes humorous.

And life in Lone Rock, Iowa, is no different.

Gene Miller was raised on his great-grandfather's farm one mile east of Lone Rock, Iowa. He is the oldest of five boys, and is co-author of *Heart to Heart: the Little Al Story*. www.littlealfoundation.org.

ODE TO A ROAD LESS TAKEN

Rae Rogers

I wonder . . . were grass roads only a phenomenon in rural Iowa, or did they exist in other states too? Both of the farm homes I remember living in had grass roads within half a mile of the farm buildings. Gypsies camped on the one near Sioux Rapids and bought fresh eggs from Mother. I was more familiar with the grass road just north of the farm, near Webb.

I faintly recall adults disdainfully referring to couples who parked on grass roads to "spoon." But there were more negative reasons those roads were sparsely used. They were absolutely impassable for cars in winter, and nearly so whenever it rained heavily. The snow remained where it fell until the spring thaw and it took a lot of warm wind and sunshine to dry the winding tracks so no tires would get stuck. If a big puddle remained for long, travelers simply drove around it and a new track developed.

My mother had another reason for not wanting to take the grassy shortcut to Spencer, the County Seat. She was deathly afraid of grasshoppers and they grew very large in Iowa! Those roads were safe havens to all kinds of insects.

So if we really needed to take the grass road shortcut, never mind that it was 90 degrees with no air conditioning, we had to ride with all the windows tightly closed. Though a straight track would have made the mile-long trip bad enough, the swoops and side tracks probably added at least another quarter mile to our misery.

The grass roads were certainly no picnic in winter, either. With no traffic to break through the drifts, walking was tedious and tiring for me as well as the neighbor kids. Actually, we only walked it once that I remember, but that was enough! The Sharp boys, the three Williams kids, and I all went sledding on the river hills near Gillett Grove one memorable winter day. I think we were all nearly teenagers, and of course we had none of the communication devices so popular with today's teens.

Someone's parent had given us a ride to the hills, about five or six miles from town, and we had a great time. We built a campfire on the flat by the river and spent a lot of energy walking up and sliding down the hills. We had heavier equipment that day than the pieces of tin or cardboard that we used during recesses on the little incline behind the schoolhouse.

Full of the food we'd brought, we were pretty tired by the time the fire died down and it was time to go home.

Then the horrible thought struck us all simultaneously. No one had arranged for a ride home! We were stuck!

So we walked. The first couple of miles after we reached the road went fairly fast. But the shortest way home led through the grass road close to the Williams' farm. Our place was another half mile past that, but the Sharp boys lived in the town of Webb, at least another mile and a half across the fields.

Of course we survived the trek. The older boys led the way, breaking a path through the hip deep snow for the girls, who pulled the lighter sleds. We were all exhausted by the time we reached our homes, but we'd learned a valuable lesson: plan ahead!

And there were no objections from any of us when the county decided to grade the road. We could always find another place to spoon!

Rae Rogers was born and raised near Webb, Iowa, in southeast Clay County, where her story took place. She and her husband owned the grocery store, Rogers' Market, in Webb for 38 years. They raised five children, who all helped in the store at one time or another. During that time she went back to college on a part-time basis, graduated from Buena Vista College in early 1971, and retired in 1990 from a career as a social worker with the Department Of Human services, and later the Northwest Iowa Mental Center.

LEAVING HOME

Joyce Jenkins

In 1940, I graduated from high school. The United States was at war in both Europe and Asia. I was working in Adams' Drugstore in Hartley, Iowa, making five dollars per week.

Sugar, meat, flour, coffee, gasoline, cigarettes and tires were rationed, old tires were recapped and we made only necessary trips to save gasoline. Points and tokens were issued for the rationed items. We planned how to use them wisely. Everyone was willing to sacrifice for the war effort.

Men between the ages of 18 to 25 were mandated to sign up for the draft. Farmers appeared before the Draft Board where it was determined who would be deferred to stay home and farm and who would go into the service. It really hit home when my cousin was called up shortly after his 18th birthday, five months before graduating from high school. After six weeks of basic training he went overseas and fought in the Battle of the Bulge. One of the first war casualties from Hartley was a classmate of mine. He was in the Air force and was shot down over the Atlantic

During the summer of 1940, I was dating Warren. He and a friend left for California that fall to find work. Families everywhere were packing up their belongings, locking up their homes and leaving their jobs and extended families as they headed for California to find work for the defense of our country. After the war ended some returned to their homes while others stayed there permanently.

Warren had offered to pay my way out to California. It had always been a desire of mine to someday make that trip. Now was my chance. But my excitement turned into a letdown after realizing I had only ten dollars to my name. Fortunately my aunt and uncle offered to loan me fifty dollars.

Two of my friends, Delores and Arlo, were planning to go to California, as Arlo had enlisted into the Navy. They were leaving within a week, and if I was going I had to make a quick decision. We contacted a private travel agency out of Sioux City. They arranged for automobile rides with people who were heading west and wished to take passengers with them to share expenses. We were able to make reservations for such a trip for $21 each.

When it came time to leave I began to get cold feet and asked myself over and over, "What am I doing?"

I can still see my mother, with that worried look and a heavy heart, knowing I would be leaving. When she handed me ten dollars, which was probably all she had, feelings of guilt consumed me.

On the drive to Sioux City I held back the tears. Then six people packed into the car, with suitcases in the trunk and two recapped tires strapped to the top. It was California or bust!

The day we arrived, Warren got his draft notice and learned he would have to report for duty in two weeks. I had to find a job. We'd heard the North American defense plant was hiring. Warren and his friend took me to Inglewood to apply. When we arrived, there was a long waiting line. I got out of the car to find a place in line and assumed Warren and his friend were going to wait for me, but they told me they had to leave. They assured me I would be okay and gave me instructions on how to find my way back to Los Angles using streetcars.

For the first time in my life I was on my own. I stood in line for what seemed like hours, and when I finally got inside I found an empty seat. I was so scared I kept cracking my gum. After a short while, a lady sitting beside me said, "Will you please either stop cracking that gum or get rid of it!"

I was embarrassed and apologized, but thought to myself that I'd never be seeing her again anyway. To my surprise we were assigned to the same job site, and eventually, we became good friends.

When called for an interview I was still nervous and scared, but when I learned that the person who interviewed me was from northwest Iowa, a new feeling of confidence came over me. The interview went well. I got a job wiring radio boxes on B25 aircraft. After two weeks of training, I started working the swing shift from 3:00 to 11:00 p.m.

Warren left for the service, and I adjusted to big city life, my job and using streetcars. Delores and I shared an apartment and worked the same shift at North American. We joined a car pool for two dollars a week. To save gas the driver dropped us off two blocks from where we lived. We walked the rest of the way through streets that at times were darkened by a blackout. By the time my first paycheck came in, all I had left to my name was fifty cents!

When Christmas came around it was my first one away from home. "I'll Be Home for Christmas" and "I'm Dreaming Of A White Christmas" played on the radio, reminding me of how far from home I was, but after Christmas I began to see familiar faces as more people from back home made their way to California.

On the Fourth of July we had a get-together that we called "Old Home Week."

In May of 1943, Warren got a furlough. We went back home to get married on the 20th of May. The next day he left for Fort Benning, Georgia, and I went back to California, to continue working until I could join him

Married men could live off base so I quit my job, went home and then took a train to Fort Benning. I was there only a short time before Warren's company was transferred to Nebraska and then to Illinois. By that time I was getting used to the moving around and making new friends.

The wives followed by train. When we reached Illinois we had to go across the border into Vincennes, Indiana, to look for housing. VACANCY signs were posted on homes where rooms or apartments were available. It was a mad rush to find something. We split up into pairs and headed off in different directions. Luckily, the first place we came upon had two one-room apartments with cooking facilities.

We bought our supplies from the PX at a discount. There was a meat market nearby, and since there was a shortage of meat I made sure to get there early before the supply was depleted. Cuts of meat were tagged to show how many ration points it took to purchase them. I saw a nice lean roast for two points, and with no hesitation I bought it.

Later, when I showed it to Warren, I said, "Look what I got for only two points!"

With a grin on his face he said, "Only two points? I can see why, it's horse meat!"

I didn't believe him, but when I put the meat in the oven and started it cooking, a strange odor slowly filled the air.

Voices down the hall called out, "What is that awful smell?"

I opened all the windows to clear the air. Later the landlady invited us for spaghetti and meatballs. We accepted her invitation, but it wasn't long before the same aroma filed the air, and again voices called out, "Oh, no, not again!"

The landlady had gone to the same meat market and had seen some nice-looking "hamburger" for only two points.

One evening she asked if we'd like to go with her to see a fortune teller. I was game, but Warren was reluctant. Finally he agreed. We drove for what seemed miles on a dirt road until we reached a little hut. A woman came to the door and invited us in. The floors were plain dirt and there was only a single kerosene lamp for light.

We all got readings. The fortune teller told me that a relative or a friend was at that very moment fighting in a battle overseas. My first thought was that it was my cousin Gale, which later proved to be correct. She told Warren that there was someone back at the base stealing from him. All the way to the car Warren kept laughing and saying, "It's all a hoax, it's all a hoax!"

The next morning, when he went to the base, he found that his locker had been broken into and his flight jacket was gone. He then changed his tune to, "I do believe!"

Two months before the war ended, orders came through that Warren's squadron was to go overseas. It was time to say good-bye to him and all the friends that I'd made. I moved back to Hartley to be near my family.

The good times, memories, and all the experiences are still with me, 60 years later. In going to California, I learned how to manage for myself in different situations, I became independent and confident, and I found a new kind of courage. I am so thankful to have had the privilege of living a part of my life during World War II, and being one of the many who sacrificed for the welfare of our country.

I hold onto these memories with tremendous pride.

Joyce (Peters) Jenkins was born and raised in Hartley, Iowa. She and her late husband, Warren, have two daughters, a son and one grandson. She was employed at the Hartley Community Memorial Hospital and Mann Nursing Wing from 1965 to 1995. She still resides in Hartley.

Photo provided by Joyce Jenkins

HOMETOWN GRATITUDE

Andrea Johnson Bean

Today, the cemetery is beautiful. It's mowed and trimmed, and flowers are reflecting off the granite tombstones as the sun dances across the spring green grass. Many American flags softly ripple in the warm breeze. Each flag is a visual reminder of those who served our country in the armed forces.

As I'm sitting here in my lawn chair, I feel like I'm a participant in a Norman Rockwell painting. I marvel at how the crowd usually consists of the same people every year. The crops are mostly planted by now and the promise of future fall harvest is in the air. This is the first visible outing for many in this rural community, after the long winter months and the hectic spring planting.

It's Memorial Day; we've come to celebrate. I feel a sense of pride, respect, gratitude and a definite love for my country, and, yes, a sense of loss. I belong here at the Fairfield Township Memorial Cemetery today. I know others who have come feel the same way. Today is a piece of America we all want to hold on to. Today is the "pause button" in our lives that takes us back in time to remember.

Time has changed a few things. We used to have the band bused out to the farm across the road, and they would march into the cemetery, playing their instruments. But we no longer have a high school in our small town of Albert City, so the community band that consists of twenty some-people of various ages are seated on folding chairs. They sit to the left of the portable Lions' Club sound system. The podium is in the front.

The ones that always touch me the most are the members of the American Legion. Each year I wonder who will replace them. The WW II veterans are getting older. Their bodies, like

147

mine, are aging. Many have passed away, but still those who are able to come do so.

I notice the Color Guard when they turn the brick corner marker. The breeze takes them back a step with the flag. Still they march on with determination and pride. We all rise to show our respect for the flag. Next comes the Honor Firing Squad, followed up by the rest of Albert City's former soldiers.

The former soldiers position themselves to the right of the speaker's podium. These days they are allowed to sit on folding chairs rather than stand at attention. Time changes things. Those in the Color Guard and Honor Firing Squad still stand. I notice that for some to stand that long is getting harder as each year passes. One can feel the reverence and pride each former soldier has for his country and the camaraderie among them. Each has experienced different opportunities, disappointments, education, jobs, respon-sibilities and life experiences, but the one thread that is stronger than the rest and ties them together is that of their service to our country.

The Girl Scouts and Boy Scouts are to the left of the podium. Their duty for the day is to place a bouquet of poppies on each of the white crosses that are marked with the name of a war. As they place the poppies by the cross, the local commander of the American Legion reads off the names of all those locally who served in that war.

The Dedication of Flags takes place next. During the ceremony, the commander reads the names of veterans who have died within the past year. As each name is read, family members walk up to one of the flagpoles in the front row. As a tribute to their loved one, a flag is dedicated and added to The Isle of Flags. Usually the flag is the same one used at the military funerals. Most of us knew those honored veterans. We might have served on committees with them, sat side by side at athletic events, shared a laugh, enjoyed pancakes at a local benefit meal, or attended church together. One can hear a pin drop as we each hold our private thoughts and emotions with a definite sense of gratitude.

Somewhere in this ceremony is a message from one of the local pastors. The community churches take turns in giving the message. Then there's the reading of the poems, "In

Flanders Fields" and "America Answers." The community band plays "God Bless America," or a rendition of other patriotic songs. Then the Honor Firing Squad steps up as the Legion commander says, "Ten-hut. Present arms. Ready . . . aim . . . fire."

In the timelessness of the morning, it is silent. Then comes the deep resonating sound of the guns firing. There's a pause, and again, "Ready . . . aim . . . fire."

I count, three times. Loud. Abrupt. Resounding.

Then, "At ease."

From the center of the ceremony comes the sound of a lone trumpeter playing "Taps." In the distant corner another single trumpet echoes the first "Taps." Softly the sound floats back.

Memorial Day ceremony at the cemetery is officially over for the year.

It's so easy to focus on the past. To think about what all those servicemen and women have done and sacrificed. The choices that they made to guard our many freedoms and give hope to the generations to come.

As I gather up my chair and other belongings and head to my vehicle, I realize that, along with the others who came today, I have been part of that hope. Memories overtake me. Wonderful memories of parents, siblings, grandparents, aunts, uncles, cousins and friends who have gone before. They've been part of that hope, too.

Then it comes to me. With the passage of time, the one thing that hasn't changed is the reason we attend the ceremony. It's our way of coming to terms with just how much each of us has been blessed and in our own small way, to say, "Thank you. Thank you for what you've given me."

Andrea (Andy) Johnson Bean is a Minnesotan (Pipestone) by birth, and an Iowan by marriage. She and her husband, Merlynn, live on his home farm in rural Albert City. She teaches art, runs a bed and breakfast, is active in local affairs and totally enjoys her role as homemaker, wife, mother and grandmother.

Photo provided by Rev. Francis Mennenga

REMEMBERING THE GREATS

Rev. Francis Mennenga

She was born August 18, 1850, in St. Joost, Ostfriesland, Germany, married Hendirk at age twenty, and arrived in America with her husband and four children in 1883. After living near relatives in Illinois for a time, the couple settled in Nebraska, and by 1910 were blessed with four more offspring. Widowed since 1920, she continued to live on the Nebraska farm located four miles southwest of Hildreth, with her eldest son, Charlie, who never married.

I did not meet Elise Christine Margarette Herren Mennenga, my great-grandmother, until 1930, the year I was born on a farm east of Huntley. My mother's death nine days after my birth brought me into the care of my father's parents. We lived on a farm three miles north of Wilcox, and were biweekly guests at my great-grandmother's table.

Elise, obviously and dutifully, loved to cook for family gatherings from the products of her large garden and the animals they raised. I especially relished the dessert always present: rice pudding with raisins. I shouldn't say that Great - Grandma was partial to me, but I supposed that under the circumstances, I received special indications that I was important in her family.

One gift I shall never forget was a pair of black wristlets with two orange lines, made to be worn under the shirtsleeves to keep cold from creeping up one's arms. The wool had come from her flock, spun on her spinning wheel, dyed and then knitted on her needles. My grandmother told me years later that some relatives were envious of the extra attention shown to me. To my knowledge the only time that my grandparents came under her discontent was when I started public school and began losing the "mother tongue."

After the sumptuous meals were served on the large dining table and the dishes done, Great-Grandmother would take her "throne" on the west wall of the dinning room, her white, rat-terrier dog beside her. Her throne was a high-backed, velvet-padded rocker with a matching footstool for her felt-slipper-covered feet.

Although all the relatives were shod in leather work or dress shoes, it was my great-grandmother's prerogative, pleasure, and preference to wear felt slippers for all occasions. She had slippers to wear in the house, another for around the farm, another for going to town, and a special pair of slippers for going to church.

It was a remarkable sight to see her with her felt slippers in her hand, for each pair had its own place and purpose. The on-the-ground slippers were changed on the porch into the going-to-town slippers. After shopping the town-slippers were transferred in the car for the to-the-farm slippers, and then again into the house-slippers at home.

This slipper exchange exercise was particularly noticeable on Sundays. Her to-the-car slippers were exchanged for the town slippers until she reached the vestibule of the church. Regardless of the occasion or the crowd, she would stop before the church's inner door to change into her church slippers, tuck the town slippers under her arm to be placed beneath the pew until the end of the service. On the way out, again the transfer from church to town got attention. Everyone seemed to know and respect her custom.

Would one call this a felt-slipper fetish? I don't know, but the origin of this custom was never associated with foot problems by the family. It was simply the usual practice of Great-Grandmother Elise.

I was over nine years old when her passing occurred. As with many in those days as now, family members, sensing the time of departure was approaching, took turns staying by Great-Grandmother's bedside around the clock.

At her bedside, as always, was her faithful pet companion. It was apparent that Tiny was aware of the situation. On the day that Great-Grandmother died, Tiny left the room, the house, and the area never to be located or found again. They had spent much time together, and it was time they left together, it seemed.

Heinrich George Marienau and his wife, Talke Catharine Pageler Marienau, lived across the section and in the same community as the Mennenga family. They were born in Germany, married in Iowa and settled four miles straight west of Hildreth, Nebraska. They parented eleven children on their farm, my father's mother among them and named her after her mother, though she never used the name "Talke," preferring Mary, her middle name.

Though I was quite young when my great-grandfather died, I remember his passing well. As his health failed his bed was moved to the living room. To make his last days more comfortable and so he could enjoy the cool air from the open window, a bed sheet was hung over the open window and sprayed, using a foot pump, with water from a tub. Because I could manipulate the pump, I was permitted to spray the sheet.

Unfortunately, it was not only Great-Grandfather who found dampness refreshing in the heat of the Nebraska summer before air-conditioning. Wasps discovered the invention and complicated the best of intentions, though I was never stung.

After Great-Grandfather died, his body was prepared and placed for viewing in his bedroom until the day of his burial.

Great-Grandmother Talke lived on the farm with her youngest son, George, and an older daughter, Emma, neither married. As with Great-Grandmother Mennenga, each Sunday family members took turns gathering at the Marienau Table. Tables were stretched and boards placed across chairs to provide extra seating on those occasions.

Because families and farms were situated closer together years ago, and transportation somewhat more limited than presently, marriages between neighboring children was not uncommon. Holiday dates and festivities had to be altered to accommodate each other's families. First and second-day Christmases were customary, stretching throughout the week until New Year's. Thanksgivings were extended to Sundays, and it was not unusual to find a windowsill seat the only place to sit for the meal.

Family closeness was natural in days past. Most communities were composed of friends and relatives, real and shirttail. Occupations were related and schedules similar for most of the residents. Separation by distance was not greatly encouraged unless one wished to be considered the family "black sheep" who would run off with a Texas gambling man.

Absence does not always make the heart grow fonder, and closeness through telephone, Internet or postal service does not improve on or measure up to the physical closeness enjoyed by families in those past years.

Great-Grandmother Talke had a medical condition that was of concern to her children. She had a tumor that covered her lap. It grew and grew until finally we children who did not know about such things were told that Grandma had her stomach "tapped," which meant drained, and her condition became closer to normal. In spite of that condition, she had wonderful knees, and a lap always ready to hold any of her grandchildren or great-grandchildren.

After her body was laid to rest in the cemetery, that sense of closeness she'd provided was not forgotten.

Times and customs have changed. New habits and traditions have replaced the old. Family togetherness may not be as essential to life today, but I cherish the old memories and love to share them with those who have missed out on a time I found to be satisfactory and joyous.

Too often the past is lost because we don't think to relay it until it's too late. A genealogist last year told me that he and his wife write a bit of history down each year as part of a Christmas gift to their children. Not a bad thought, and one I too have begun to practice. Hopefully others will benefit and follow suit.

Rev. Francis Mennenga, retired Lutheran Pastor after 50 years of ministry in Texas congregations (Dallas, Lubbock, Hamilton and Whitney) and Hartley, Iowa. He and his wife are presently living in Hewitt, Texas, a suburb of Waco.

NOVEMBER 22, 1963

Karen Laughlin

Four days after my sixteenth birthday I stood among a crowd of teenage girls. The din of their chattering voices filled the girl's large restroom at Thomas Jefferson High School, in Cedar Rapids, Iowa. I was on my half-hour lunch break and had finished eating. The wall-to-wall mirror stretched over the long-row sinks. I combed my bleached-blonde, page-boy-styled hair and then straightened my pink cashmere sweater and matching pink pleated skirt. Next I began applying Lush Pink lipstick to my lips and cheeks.

Girls pushed and shoved like a herd of gazelles at a watering hole to get to the mirrors and sinks in the restroom.

We were baby boomers and seemed to do everything in overcrowded groups. In the mirror's reflection I saw a girl hurriedly enter the room and shove her way into the middle of the shifting crowd.

She shouted above the din, "The President's been shot!"

Everyone turned toward her in shocked silence. The expression on her face was normal, as if it were a bad joke.

I sarcastically replied, "Ya, sure."

She looked at me. Tears welled up in her eyes and her voice choked. "No, it's true. Go out in the hall. The principal's on the P.A."

We stood stone still for a moment more, as the reality of what she'd said and what it meant sank in. Then, in disbelief, we quietly filed out into the hall.

On the public address speaker our principal was repeating the news that President John F. Kennedy had been shot in Dallas, Texas, and had been rushed to the hospital. All students and teachers were to immediately return to their scheduled classrooms and stay there until further notice.

The shuffle of feet on the marble floors was the only sound in the packed halls. The usual noisy hassle of maneuvering

155

through baby-boomer crowds was gone. People formed polite lines on both sides of the hall and slowly made their way back to classrooms.

My knees wobbled like Jell-O and I stared at the floor as I went back to biology class. We sat at long black-topped tables in pairs. My partner was John, who was from England. No one spoke.

The public address speaker sputtered on again. The principal announced that he was going to let us listen to CBS radio. Walter Cronkite's somber but professional voice came over the P.A. To me, it sounded reassuring. The class listened in silence as Mr. Cronkite recapped the day's events up to the shooting and what had happened after. He described the scene in vivid detail . . . the motorcade, the happy, cheering crowds, the shots ringing out, people falling to the ground, the President's car speeding away, and the faces of weeping people everywhere.

My stomach churned. My lunch didn't want to stay put, but I willed it down. Head bowed, I sat with my hands folded in my lap.

Tragic death hadn't touched my young life until then. My body seemed separated from my mind as I listened to the radio, unable to process the full effect of this terrible event.

Walter Cronkite's voice remained controlled as he announced, "President John F. Kennedy died at . . ."

The room erupted in the sound of uncontrolled weeping. Gasping cries of, "No!" rang out. Every girl was sobbing . . . and most of the boys, too, though some tried to fight back their tears.

I covered my face with my hands and sobbed. I peeked through my fingers at our teacher, Mr. Cameron. He stood at the front of the class, his hands behind him, with a lost expression on his face. It looked as though he didn't know what to do either. Maybe he was at a loss of how to handle all these kids.

Loneliness overwhelmed me. I was on my own in this time of pain and confusion.

John turned to me and asked, "Why is everyone crying?"

I dropped my hand and turned toward him, my mouth open. "The President is dead," I whispered.

The whole scene seemed surreal. President Kennedy and his wife, Jackie, were so young and vibrant. Then I remembered their two young children, Caroline and John. My heart broke for them as a fresh wave of sorrow swept over me and tears flowed down my checks. I grabbed a tissue from my purse as my sinuses released their contents.

What idiot would want to kill a man who'd meant so much to his family and the world? My young mind was numb and couldn't wrap it around the awful truth. So many thoughts and questions swirled around in my head. Our president was gone. It had been exciting having this young family in the White House. My parent's hadn't voted for him, but once elected he was *their* president.

I was crazy about horses and jumped them, just like Mrs. Kennedy did. Caroline had her pony, Macaroni, at the White House. I, too, had had a pony when I was her age. They'd seemed like a regular family . . . only richer.

Now it was all over. It had never dawned on me that our country might be unsafe. Now Vice President Johnson would take over. I had learned that in government class.

The principal broke in on the P.A. again, interrupting Walter Cronkite, and told us that school would be dismissed soon. The school buses would arrive shortly for those who rode them. School was over. It would be announced on TV and radio newscasts when school would start again.

I made my way over to the other building where my locker was. Kids exchanged hushed whispers as they hurriedly departed. Many openly wept. Only wet, somber faces passed me in the hall.

I saw a friend. We hadn't been talking to each other for a week . . . some silly argument. Our eyes met. We smiled sadly at each other and said, "Hi." Whatever disagreement we'd had faded. It wasn't important now.

As I headed for the school bus I felt separated from my body. I was walking, but I never understood how I got from point A to point B.

The school bus had to stop and pick up children at the junior high and elementary schools. No one spoke. I heard every shift of the buses gears and felt every bump on the road. My senses seemed heightened and dulled at the same time.

I arrived home to an empty house. My parents both worked off the farm. My mother worked for KCRG-TV. I didn't know until later that evening that her accounting department was frantically reworking accounts for advertisers. The only three national networks had gone to full coverage of the assassination.

After changing my clothes I went out to check the animals, which was my usual routine. I muddled my way through my chores, crying the whole time.

When I was finished, I went back to the house and flipped on the television. There it all was, in black and white, the scene that had earlier been described on the radio.

Over the next few days I sat sobbing on the sofa, watching TV. The horror of those moments had been recorded and would be forever replayed, again and again: Mrs. Kennedy leaning toward her husband after the first shot, then the second shot and the President's head exploding in her face. She crawled back onto the trunk of the convertible as it sped forward.

Later the President's coffin was hoisted aboard the airplane, his widow at its side, for the long flight back to Washington, DC. Aboard the plane, Vice President Johnson, was sworn in as president, while a bewildered Mrs. Kennedy looked on.

The media reported that she was still wearing her blood-stained pink suit.

The funeral: Dignitaries walking up the avenue behind Mrs. Kennedy; Caroline kneeling at the coffin, kissing the flag; John-John saluting his father's coffin as it passed in front of him. The incessant drumbeat of the funeral procession vibrated to my core and I thought I'd never get that beat out of my head.

I watched as Lee Harvey Oswald, was shot on live television. Would the killing never stop?

At sixteen I learned that life isn't fair, and sometimes it's downright brutal. And that no one is guaranteed all the time in the world. After that day, I never took life for granted again.

Karen Laughlin is a freelance writer and lives on her farm outside of Cedar Rapids, Iowa. At one time she was a breeder/trainer of horses and a dealer in horse books.

Photo provided by Ruth Jochims

SCRAPBOOKS

Ruth Jochims

On weekend afternoons, my father frequently asked my sister and me if we'd like to go for a ride. We always did. My sister, Doris, and I loved to get away from the bustling city of Des Moines. Dad was adventuresome. He enjoyed looking for fun places to hike. We never knew where we'd end up. Some times Mom would go along for the ride, but she wasn't a hiker, so more often than not she'd stay home and take a nap or catch up on her sewing.

One day, while on one of these outings with my father, we traveled past vast cornfields, and memories of my earlier home in the Pacific Northwest flashed through my mind.

"I hate looking at cornfields! I wish we could move back to Oregon!" I whined.

Dad didn't say much. He just listened to my complaints. Sometimes he'd start singing. As we joined in, it put me in a better mood.

When the car stopped in a wooded area, we jumped out. Dad found a walking stick, and off I went, up the trail. I had no patience for slow pokes and liked to run ahead, but Dad called for me to wait for them.

As we hiked, Dad stopped to look at the wildflowers. He carried a flower book with him, but he usually knew the names of most of them. He'd been a schoolteacher, and to our childish minds, he appeared to know everything!

Some times Dad took us to the Ledges State Park near Boone. On those occasions Mom packed a picnic lunch and came along. She didn't hike though. She was content to just sit and enjoy nature while the rest of us hiked.

Ledges Park, which was so enchanting, was my favorite hiking place. The gigantic hills seemed like mountains, challenging to climb, especially for one who was afraid of heights! Once I climbed up a steep rocky trail and was afraid to go back down. Dad came to my rescue and helped me down. I was a clumsy kid, and falling was one of my fears.

As we climbed near the top, the panoramic view took my breath away. Far below, the creek that we loved to wade in, searching for tadpoles, looked so tiny from where we stood.

Our stomach-rumblings reminded us it was time to start down. Mom had laid out the lunch on a picnic table near the creek. There were baked beans, potato salad, watermelon, and shoestring potatoes, as well as sandwiches, cookies, and a jug of Kool-Aid. As we ate, the birds and chipmunks begged for handouts. We laughed at their antics.

One day, before we went on one of our excursions, Dad had a surprise for us. He gave us each a scrapbook. Dad had a big scrapbook of his own, full of pressed wildflowers. He had labeled them with their scientific names, names he'd learned by studying their petals in his flower book.

This new hobby was fun at first, but I grew tired of it quickly. I'd rather be hiking than trying to figure out the names of flowers. Dad also had us study the names of trees, which I went along with to please him.

When we weren't studying flowers and trees, we looked for rocks. Doris was a rock collector. It was fun looking for pretty rocks for her collection.

I don't remember when we stopped collecting flowers and leaves. Perhaps it was when I went away to school. At any rate, that hobby went by the wayside.

Dad did other fun things with us. Sometimes he took us to the amusement park. We loved the rides, though I was afraid of the roller coaster. Dad finally coaxed me to go with him. He held on to me as my body tried to rise up out of my seat. Since Dad was with me, it was fun! He helped me master many of my fears.

Years later, as I was rummaging around in the basement, I came across my flower scrapbook. I leafed through the pages, awakening memories of long ago. I also found my high school scrapbook, with pictures of days that seem foreign to me now.

Ah . . . there was the picture of Doris and me playing a piano duet. We were so skinny back then!

I stood there, holding the scrapbook and reminiscing. As Bailey, my furry cat rubbed against my legs, I shut the book. I have other hobbies now.

Ironically, my Dad and my sister moved back to Oregon, the place I had longed to be. I ended up in the small town of Spencer, Iowa, a great town with everything I need. I raised two daughters here. One liked hiking, and the other didn't. One daughter liked to run ahead, just as I had. They grew up in a small town with cornfields all around.

In spite of my dislike of cornfields, I wouldn't be able to eat hot, buttery ears of corn without them!

Ruth Jochims lives in Spencer, Iowa, with her husband, Victor, and a spoiled black cat. She has two daughters and five grandchildren. She is a retired nurse's aide, plays the piano and organ, and most of all, loves to write.

A BOX FULL OF MEMORIES

By Delpha Chouanard

It was a March day in Northern Minnesota. I cursed the snow that slowed the movements of my second-hand boots and winced at the sleet that stung my cheeks. I led six of my siblings out of the woods toward home. The usual signs of spring were absent, as though Mother Winter had thrown her white blanket over the land, tucked it in, and kissed it goodnight. The birds remained south and the flowers waited for a hotter sun to melt the blanket of snow and awaken them. After a long cold winter the harbingers of spring waited for their chance to come forth and erase winter's memory.

When the roads were snowy or muddy, our bus driver, who was also the fire chief and town policeman, dropped my siblings and me off at the county road. Since it was a long walk from the county road to our farmhouse, we always took the shortcut through the woods. On that day the trees provided some protection, but we were soaked by the time we stepped into the kitchen door.

The scent of fresh bread reached our nostrils. I took in a deep breath to smell the delicious snack before I removed my winter gear and sat down to eat. After we enjoyed a healthy helping of butter on our bread, my sisters and I ran upstairs to play with our paper dolls.

"Mine's all cut up," I said holding up the Sears and Roebuck catalog while I peered at my sisters through the holey pages. We giggled as Vivian dumped her shoebox of paper dolls on the worn rug. We'd spent the last six months carefully cutting from the 1952 spring clothing catalogs.

"Mom's gonna get the new spring catalogs any day and we can have her old fall ones," I said as I dumped my shoebox on the floor. I watched Jean's petite hands work as she sorted through her box and carefully laid out each family member's clothes.

"Delpha, I get the Sears Catalog this time, right?" Jean asked.

"Yep, and I get the Spiegel and Vivian gets Montgomery Ward's," I said. It worked out perfectly. Mom had three girls and she received three catalogs every six months. We rotated the catalogs among us.

We heard a truck struggling on the snow as it drove up the road. Our eyes met for a second before we ran to the window. We held our breaths as we watched Dad pull up to the side of the house and then squealed when we saw his arms loaded with mail. Our harbinger of spring had finally arrived.

We bolted down the stairs into the kitchen, where we stood straight, smiles on our faces, and waited.

"Looks like we got the new catalogs," Dad said giving us a wink.

"All right," said Mom, "you girls know where to get the old ones."

We sure did. With scissors in hand we ran straight for Mom's side table.

"Don't run with scissors, girls!" Mom yelled.

That night and for many nights after we sat down on the floor, full from supper, and meticulously cut out people and clothes from the catalogs. We started with the underwear pages, where we each picked out the perfect doll. I chose the woman with the brown, naturally curly hair and deep blue eyes.

We found the most stylish dresses in every color imaginable, with matching hats, shoes, and hand bags. We cut to the sound of banging pots and pans, cowboy and Indian war-whoops, and *The Amos and Andy Show* mixed with knee-slapping laughter.

When I played, I transformed myself into my doll. I was not the Delpha who wore dresses made from flour sacks. Nor was I the Delpha who slept in uncomfortable curlers at night in a desperate attempt to make my straight hair curly. I was the Delpha who ordered chiffon dresses and silk stoles from catalogs. The catalog Delpha's biggest worry was to pick the right dress for the right occasion.

"Hey, girls," Mom said as she wiped her hands on her apron. "Remember to put your old catalogs in the outhouse. We're running out of paper."

After five months of cutting, our shoeboxes overflowed. Summer turned into fall and fall turned into tragedy. In late September our bus driver was called to a fire. We waited for a substitute driver, and as we reached the county road I saw that it was *our* house engulfed in flames.

The immense fire seemed to wrap its hot tongue around the melting shingle siding. It reminded me of a large marshmallow burning in the campfire ashes. Only this was not a sweet sugary smell; it was the smell of burning memories.

My first thought was for my Mom and two younger brothers. *Were they safe?* As we walked closer to the house I saw my Mom and brothers amongst the crowd that had gathered. I was relieved to see everyone was okay, but the tears still came. We didn't have much, but everything we did have was consumed by this fire. Our paper dolls that we worked so hard on were gone.

After hearing about the family of eleven who lost all to a fire, the community pitched in with clothes, food, and other needs. Our family was split into different homes for about a month before we moved into a new farmhouse. My sisters and I stayed with my best friend. We wore her clothes and despite everything, we had a great time. It was like a never-ending slumber party with my best friends.

The following March, the snow still covered the ground, the birds still remained south, and the flowers still lay sleeping. Dad came in to the new house with our cherished harbingers of spring under his arm. He said with a wink, "Looks like the new catalogs are here."

We giggled and shook with excitement. It was time to rebuild our paper doll collection; just as, with the help of family and friends, we'd rebuilt our lives. It took me a while to realize that it wasn't memories that had burned that autumn day. What had burned were old shingles, boards and furniture.

Memories last forever.

Delpha Chouanard lives in Deephaven, Minnesota, with her husband, Harvey. She enjoys quilting and spending time with her six grandchildren.

THE BACK PORCH

By Ronda Armstrong

In the 1950s and 1960s, I grew up in a white, green-shuttered corner house in Emporia, Kansas. The enclosed back porch had windows across three sides. To the north we looked out over the spiraea bushes, and the trimmed hedge that bordered the yard, catching a view of the houses along Seventh Street from Oak Street to Chestnut Street. On the east, we eyed the backyard: the sandbox, the swing, the double garage, the flower beds, and the redbud trees beyond the cemented driveway. Looking south: a sprawling garden covered an entire lot where, during garden season, flowers, fruits, and vegetables grew in abundance.

We called it the back porch but, as a busy room with many functions, it really deserved a more honored name. Our family entered our home through the door on the back porch; neighbors and friends did the same. From the driveway we opened the metal gate and walked on the sidewalk across the yard, up the three steps, and through the door to where the back porch welcomed everyone and whispered the last goodbyes when we left.

Sometimes we had more excitement than expected, like the evening Ike, one of our cats, rushed in after my dad and the door slammed on his tail. After the incident and medical attention, Ike sat on the porch sulking. He wasn't happy—embarrassed, most likely—about the huge white bandage wrapped around his fluffy, injured tail. Another year bluebirds built a nest just outside the porch. They created quite a racket when they squawked at my mom and tried to peck her as she went in and out.

Since my dad owned a sand and gravel company, a phone had been installed right inside the back door so my parents could answer business calls when they worked in the yard or the garden. A small ledge under the black wall-phone served as a message center, always stocked with a notepad and tin can stuffed with pens and pencils. In later years, fewer business calls came to our home. Still, we kept the phone on the porch. It belonged there, along with the petite walnut rocker that sat beside it.

When my grandmother visited us, she rocked in the chair while she talked on the phone to her friend, Ingabo, who, until her retirement, sold hats at Newman's Department Store. My mom rested in the chair when she made calls between household or gardening tasks.

Often I claimed this spot, phone at my ear, chatting with my friends and planning activities.

The ironing board was always up along the north side of the porch. The iron sat on it, ready to be plugged in. Something always needed ironing—a dress, an apron, a pair of slacks or shorts, or a piece of a sewing project. While we ironed we gazed at the yard, nature's gifts, the street, and the passersby. This ritual exuded peace, a sense of slowing down, of taking the pulse of the season and of the neighborhood.

A square table, covered with a flowered oilcloth, sat in the southeast corner. It acted as a catchall for small garden tools, gloves thrown off, a bit of fresh-picked produce. We also fed the cat on it to keep the dog from snatching the cat's food. The dog ate on the porch floor, his domain. This routine remained in force long after the dog died, even though our last cat was so arthritic she couldn't jump up on the table. She waited patiently on the floor until my mother, also ridden with arthritis, reached down to gently lift her up.

Once a year the corner table showcased several boxes of peonies in foil-wrapped tin-can vases, ready to deliver to the cemeteries for Memorial Day. Before we loaded them in the car, we paused to look at the bouquets of brilliant glory. This pause reflected a bit of reverence, of remembrance in the comfort of home, during which the porch seemed to pour its blessings over the bunches of peonies to christen them for sacred duty.

By the time I was a teenager an upright freezer stood in the southeast corner of the porch, by the entrance to the kitchen. Inside its doors, stored in old coffee cans, my sister and I found our mom's sought-after chocolate-chip cookies, as mouth watering as a first-prize winner at the fair. From time to time we'd ask her if she had a secret to her cookie recipe. She'd always say, "A secret? I don't have a secret, just my trusty oven and the *Better Homes and Gardens Cookbook* recipe."

We believed her caring touch made the difference.

Our family also rifled through the freezer to unearth the last of the year's frozen asparagus, lima beans, black raspberries, or other items required for our favorite meals. When tantalizing aromas greeted us as we opened the porch door, smiles inched across our faces as we inhaled a big whiff in anticipation of the taste of home.

The storage closet, in the northwest corner, hinted of mystery. The clothes hook, where we hung clothes for ironing, rested on the outside of the closet door. Inside, a clothes rod ran across one side. It held aprons, gardening jackets, work shirts, and coats. The red paint-splattered stepladder, often with the meat grinder still attached, sat in the middle. When we didn't know where else to look for an item we sought, we unlatched the closet door, pulled the light chain, and searched the shelves, boxes, and tin cans of accumulated odds and ends, each with its own story.

The back porch radiated the soul of our home, transforming it into a priceless asset. When we returned from our journeys it gave our family and our guests a hearty welcome, that first sense of the familiar, of having arrived at the place called home. And, when it was time to go, we caught our breath and gathered our strength in the sanctuary of the porch before we traveled down the back steps and into the world once again.

The porch anchored us, day or night.

My mother dropped onto the porch rocker on the June morning we came home from the hospital, after my father died. Buttressed by the comfort of the porch, she phoned her sister, her brother, and her best friends to share the sad news. Years later, when my sister, my husband, and I were summoned to the hospital at midnight for my mother's final hours, the outside light of the same porch shone in the bleak darkness of the bitter-cold January night.

After my mother died in 1988, our family sold the home. Before we left for good we stepped outside, where my husband snapped a photo of my sister, my aunts, a family friend, and me. The snapshot captured the back porch behind us, standing tall and proud, a fitting witness to decades of family life and timeless memories.

Ronda Armstrong, a native Kansan, lives with her husband and two cats in Des Moines, Iowa. She and her husband enjoy ballroom dancing. Ronda's stories have appeared in *Chicken Soup for the Soul* and *The Des Moines Register*, as well as the second Midwest anthology, *Knee High by the Fourth of July*.

Photo provided by Ronda Armstrong

COMING IN 2011

Make Hay While the Sun Shines
*Fourth in the Series of Stories about Growing Up in and
Around Small Towns in the Midwest*

Word Count: 500 to 1600

Send submissions to:

Jean@midwestwriter.com

or

Shapato Publishing
PO Box 476
Everly, Iowa 51338

ORDER FORM

Mail Order Form to: Shapato Publishing
PO Box 476
Everly, IA 51301

Knee High by the Fourth of July:
More Stories of Growing Up in and
Around Small Towns in the Midwest $14.00 ea
ISBN: 978-0982105870   + .98 sales tax ea

Walking Beans Wasn't Something You
Did With Your Dog:
Stories of Growing Up in and Around Small
Towns in the Midwest $14.00 ea
ISBN: 978-0982105801   + .98 sales tax ea

S&H per quantity: $3.00 for 1 – 3 books

Enclosed is check or money order for: $_____

Payable to **Shapato Publishing**.

NAME: _____

ADDRESS:_____

Or order safely online at:
www.ShapatoPublishing.com

ORDER FORM

Mail Order Form to: Shapato Publishing
PO Box 476
Everly, IA 51301

The Earth Abides
A Collection of Poetry and Personal Essays
By Betty Taylor
ISBN: 978-0982105894

$14.00 ea
+ .98 sales tax ea

Good Fences
By Marshall Crane
ISBN: 978-0982105887

$14.95 ea
+1.05 sales tax ea

Life with my Wife
The Memoir of an Imperfect Man
By Roger Stoner
ISBN: 978-0982699256

$14.95
+1.05 sales tax ea

S&H per quantity: $3.00 for 1 – 3 books

Enclosed is check or money order for: $_____

Payable to **Shapato Publishing**.

NAME: _____

ADDRESS:_____

Or order safely online at:
www.ShapatoPublishing.com